FINANCIAL TRANSACTIONS OF THE WHOLESALE DISTRIBUTOR

■■■■■■■■

by
Dr. Don A. Rice
Professor Emeritus of Industrial Distribution

■ ■ ■

Fourth Edition

■ ■ ■

Published by
DARCO Press
P.O. Box 5550
Bryan, Texas
Phone/Fax (409) 776-1516

■ ■ ■ Dedication ■ ■ ■

This book is dedicated first to my Lord and Savior Jesus Christ, the source of eternal salvation and the provider of all good and wonderful things.

Secondly it is dedicated to three business associates whom I consider to be among my personal friends, colleagues and mentors.

Gary Buffington, Executive Vice President, Industrial Distribution Association

Andrea Herbert, Editorial Director, *Electrical Wholesaling*

Gordon Graham, Consultant and fellow Christian

■ ■ ■ Acknowledgements ■ ■ ■

The writer wishes to express appreciation to the many individuals and associations whose members assisted and contributed to the completion of this text.

Special thanks is extended to David Meredith, Vice President of Summit Electric Supply for his continual encouragement and personal commitment to the furtherance of the education of people who will invest their skills and knowledge in the industry.

Gratitude is extended to Bob Merson, Chairman of the Board, Southern Electric Supply Company, for his careful consideration and suggestions concerning the text.

Appreciation is also expressed to these trade publications, *Electrical Wholesaling, Supply House Times and Industrial Distribution* for the availability of resource information.

The writer would also like to acknowledge and express appreciation to the staff of the following trade associations and their members who provided technical information and assistance:

American Supply Association

American Supply and Machinery Manufacturers Association

Associated Equipment Distributors

Fluid Power Distributors Association

Industrial Distribution Association

National Association of Electrical Distributors

National Associate of Wholesaler-Distributors

National Electronic Distributors Association

National Welding Supply Association

Power Transmission Distributors Association

Thank you is also extended to the following individuals who proofed and commented on the data:

Ron Schriebman, National Association of Wholesaler-Distributors

Ken Plough, President, Plough Electric, San Francisco, CA

David Peebles, Ferguson Enterprise, Newport News, VA

John O'Reilly, *Supply House Times*

Dr. Demo Stavros, Eastern Michigan University, Ypsilanti, MI

Gordon Graham, Consultant, Dallas, TX

A warm, heart felt thanks is expressed to my wife Sara and our three children, Rhonda, Dan and Dawna for their patience and understanding of the time I spent with this book instead of with them during the development of this material.

A special appreciation is also extended to all the Industrial Distribution students at Texas A&M University who helped proof the material.

**THIS BOOK IS PROTECTED BY INTERNATIONAL COPYRIGHTS
AND MAY NOT BE REPRODUCED IN ANY FORM
UNDER PENALTY OF LAW**

© 1982, 1986, 1989, 1994, 1997. Dr. Don A. Rice, dba, DARCO Press. All rights are expressly reserved. No portion of this book may be reproduced. The reproduction or utilization of this work in any form or by an electronic, mechanical, or other means not known or hereafter invented, including xerography, photo-copying, or recording in any information storage or retrieval system is forbidden without the expressed written permission of the publisher.

ISBN 1-881154-04-1

Manufactured in the United States of America

©1997, Don A. Rice dba DARCO Press. All Rights Reserved.
COPYRIGHT LAW MAKES IT ILLEGAL TO COPY THIS BOOK IN ANY FORM.

■ ■ ■ Preface ■ ■ ■

The materials in this text are presented in an effort to enlighten its readers concerning the proper methods to utilize in teaching and understanding percentages, discounts, gross margins, company profits, and other financial transactions of the wholesaler distributor.

The concepts included here, though elementary in nature, are essential to the profitable and efficient operation of all wholesale businesses.

The correct procedure to use in calculating percentages is discussed both as a review and as a practical guide for the use of percentages in the wholesale distributorship.

A concept commonly misunderstood by persons unfamiliar with the wholesale distribution of goods is the proper method to use in the calculation of percent margin and percent profit. This is especially true when calculating the margin and selling price from a known cost of goods. The chapter which discusses these subjects should correct these misconceptions and leave the reader with a thorough understanding of how to calculate them and why the method being described is correct.

Another topic discussed in this text is the use of various discounts common to the wholesale business, particularly trade and cash discounts.

This text is not meant to be an exclusive work on all of the financial transactions of the wholesaler-distributor but is limited to the basic functions involved in buying and selling goods and services. It is primarily designed for the newly employed. However, more experienced persons may refresh their prior learning by quick applications of the principles demonstrated.

■ ■ ■ Table of Contents ■ ■ ■

1. **Employees & Profit Knowledge** 3
2. **Terminology**
   2.1 Explanation of Common Terms 9
   2.2 Terms of Sale 12
   2.3 Financial Terms 15
3. **Percentages in Wholesaling**
   3.1 Calculating the Percent 23
   3.2 Calculating the Percentage 26
   3.3 Calculating the Rate 29
   3.4 Calculating the Base 32
   3.5 Percent of Change Between Numbers 35
4. **Trade Discounts**
   4.1 Trade Discounts 43
   4.2 Simplified Method 46
   4.3 Multiple Discounts: Using Multiplying Factors 48
   4.4 Table of Multiplier Factors 50
   4.5 Payment for Services Rendered 55
   4.6 Profit Eroded by Additional Discounts 57
5. **Cash Discounts**
   5.1 General Cash Discount Terminology 59
   5.2 Common Types of Cash Discounts 61
   5.3 Why Cash Discounts are Offered 63
   5.4 The Importance of Taking the Cash Discount 66
   5.5 The Argument: Do We Discount or Pay Late? 70
   5.6 Discounting Makes Money Easier Than
       Increasing Sales 73
   5.7 Passing Through the Discount 75
   5.8 Cash Discounts and Extend Dating 76

6. **Markups** 81
   6.1 How to Calculate Percent Gross Margin
        When Percent Markup is Known 83
   6.2 How to Calculate Percent Markup When
        Percent Gross Margin is Known 85
   6.3 How to Calculate Percent Markup When
        the COGS and Selling Price are Known 88
   6.4 How to Calculate Selling Price from COGS
        Using the Divisor Principle 89
   6.5 How to Calculate Selling Price from COGS
        Using the Multiplier Principle 92
   6.6 How to Calculate Multiple Markups from Cost 94
   6.7 Trade Pricing 98

7. **Interest**
   7.1 Simple Interest Formula 101
   7.2 Single Payment Notes 103
   7.3 Add-On Interest 106

8. **Return on Investment** 111

9. **Answer Key** 117

10. **The Author** 141

11. **Order Form**

*Financial Transactions
of the
Wholesale Distributor*

A Book for New Employees

Chapter 1

Employees and Profit Knowledge

The renowned football coach of the famous Green Bay Packers, Vince Lombardi, concluded that football games were not won consistently on fancy plays, but on basic skills of blocking and tackling. Though Green Bay seldom lost under his direction, when they did, during Monday's practice they always went *back to basics*, blocking and tackling.

As the economy continually fluctuates, it is necessary for wholesale distributors to train their employees on the basics. One of the most basic wholesaling principles is understanding profit and the difference between gross margin and net profit. It has been the author's experience during years of teaching in industry that many employees do not understand and are shocked when they learn this difference. The difference is great.

Let's review the relationship between gross margin and net profit using the following example. A wholesaler pays $75.00 for an item (the cost of goods to be sold). The wholesaler then sells the item and invoices the customer for $100.00.

The gross margin, *WHICH IS ALWAYS CALCULATED ON THE SELLING PRICE*, is 25%, ($100.00 X .25 = $25.00). If the selling price is used to indicate the amount we invoiced the customer, then the selling price minus the cost of goods sold is equal to the margin ($100.00 − $75.00 = $25.00 = gross margin).

The dollar amount we pay for an item to be sold including the freight is called the cost of goods sold or COGS. The money we received from the customer for the product is called the net selling price. The difference between the selling price and the COGS is known by several different terms, all meaning about the same thing. The difference is actually the margin, but is often called gross margin, profit margin, or gross profit margin. You should know that all of these terms relate to the difference between the selling price and the cost of goods sold. These terms are used interchangeably in industry. However, because of the misunderstandings caused by the use of the term "gross profit" we will restrict our use, and suggest that you do, to the term "gross margin" or simply "margin".

Many employees erroneously think the $25.00 in the example given above is profit. This is a terrible misconception. The $25.00 is the gross margin and must be spent to cover the expense of employee wages and benefits, purchasing, inventory, selling, warehousing, credit, record keeping, sales commissions, cost of locating and picking up items that have been purchased locally, transportation, utilities, taxes, and other administrative costs. This will consume about $23.00 of the $25.00 of gross margin. After the wholesaler has paid all of these expenses, he/she finally has net profit after tax of one or two dollars per hundred dollar sale, assuming the expenses mentioned did not consume the entire gross margin. If the expenses are greater than the margin, the company will experience a loss on the sale.

The majority of the gross margin dollars is spent on personnel. A rule of thumb is that one half of the gross margin dollars will be used to pay employee wages and benefits. In the example given above, $12.50 of the $25.00 margin went to the distributor's employees for wages and benefits. Few employees really understand the significance of the expense their employer incurs in providing their job opportunities. In addition to their wages, the employer also bears the cost of benefits such as workman's compensation insurance, a portion of the social security taxes, paid holidays, paid vacations, retirement benefits, illness, jury duty, bonuses, profit share, supplemental insurance premiums, and other expenses.

However, it is natural for employees to relate primarily to the amount of their take home payroll check (after the deductions) because this is the amount which the employee can spend for the necessities of life. However, we should understand that the employer is spending a great deal more than even the *gross* amount shown on our check stub. We should realize and appreciate the total contribution of the wholesaler to our overall financial well being. For example, for every $100.00 which you take home, the company will spend approximately $166.00.

Of this amount, $43.00 was withheld and sent to the government to cover the federal income and social security taxes. In addition, the employer must pay at least a matching portion of the social security and usually also freely provides paid holidays, vacation, workman's compensation, health insurance, etc., amounting to an additional 14% of the employee's wages. This is money the employer spends, but employees never see. This means that in reality, for every $100.00 which you receive in wages which you can spend, the employer spent $166.00. This is about 40% more than what you take home.

When the cost of goods consumes approximately $75.00 of a $100.00 sale, this leaves only $25.00 to cover expenses and profits. With employee wages and benefits consuming approximately half of the gross margin and the expense of operating the business consuming the other half, such as rent, utilities, telephone service, local taxes, interest, delivery, and postage, to name only a few, it is no wonder that the net profit which remains after tax on a $100.00 sale is only about $1.50 to $2.00.

Consequently, you should understand the critical nature of the costs of doing business when the profits are so small. For example, one additional long distance phone call which costs only four dollars will kill all of the profit on a $200.00 sale. It is even worse when you consider employee theft, damaged merchandise, wrong shipments, and returned goods.

For example, let's say that an employee drops, runs a fork lift through, or otherwise damages or steals a $300.00 item from the warehouse. If the pretax profits for this company are 3 percent of sales, then it takes $10,000.00 in new, additional sales just to break even on the $300.00 loss ($300.00 ÷ .03 = $10,000.00). If the company can generate $10,000.00 in new sales they will reach the break-even point (the point at which they neither make nor lose any money, but simply cover their cost of goods sold and the cost of doing business). Few people realize how devastating these small numbers are to the overall profitability of the company. The reason it takes so many additional dollars of sales is because the profits for the average distributor are so small. Therefore, it is the responsibility of every one of us to keep the profits up by keeping the costs down.

Let's take a moment and define what we mean by profit. Profit is calculated as the excess of revenues over expenditures. Mathematically, this definition is correct. In addition, profit is the *reward* received by an individual or corporation for *taking a financial risk* and applying sound business practices. Profit is absolutely essential to any company operating in a free enterprise economy that plans to continue in business.

The profit motive for employees is simple to understand. Let's suppose you have the opportunity to work for either of two different companies, one which is reasonably profitable and one which makes little or no profit. Let's look at several common characteristics which show the relationship between the two.

Characteristics Compared

Marginally Profitable Companies May:

Pay low salaries

Have few, if any, company benefits

Operate under unsafe or hazardous working conditions

Operate using inefficient or dangerous equipment

Provide no community support

Offer no job security

Reasonably Profitable Companies May:

Pay reasonable salaries

Have good company benefits

Provide safe working conditions

Operate cost-effective equipment

Support the local community with funds

Provide job security

Obviously, most employees would prefer to be employed by the more profitable company. If you do, then you have the responsibility to do everything within your power to improve the company's profit position. This would include coming to work every day and being on time, giving a day's work for a day's pay, working effectively and efficiently, helping cut operating expenses by working smarter, generating cost savings ideas, writing them down and passing them on to management, and being a "part of the team" where everybody works together to make the company a profitable and enjoyable place to work.

An employee should show initiative and should not hesitate to make suggestions for improvement in efficiency and cost-saving when the employee sees how this can be accomplished. Do not sit back and complain about how things are being run. Make suggestions to your supervisor about things you believe to be cost and time-saving ideas.

In this light, employees should remember that job security comes from profitability. If a company is profitable, it will make good job opportunities available. However, *profitability is always dependent upon customer satisfaction*, while service is based on employee performance. Without customer satisfaction there are no sales and, consequently, no profit and no jobs.

Every financial transaction of the distributor is conducted for the purpose of enhancing the small profits earned. The better understanding you have of these transactions, the better decisions you will make and both you and your company will reap the rewards.

Before we go any further with our presentation, it is necessary that we explain the terminology we will use in the following chapters so that we have a common understanding of what is being discussed. We will start by explaining the various terms and words associated with financial transactions which occur in the wholesale distribution business.

Chapter 2

Terminology

2.1 Explanation of Common Terms

You may already be familiar with most of the financial terms used in the wholesale industry. If so, scan these rapidly to see that the way they are used in this text is compatible with your prior experience. If you are not fully acquainted with these terms, the brief description and explanation of how they are used in this industry will be beneficial to your thorough understanding of the other materials presented.

Wholesaler/Distributor

The wholesaler/distributor is identified primarily by the functions performed and not the products being sold. The wholesaler is a vital link in what is known as the "channel of distribution" which represents all of the entities required to move a product from where it is manufactured to the point where it is used. The industrial distributor is primarily involved where a "high service level" must be maintained. The industrial distributor will generally buy and sell both technical products as well as commodity-type products. Distributor may be identified by the following characteristics:

1. Maintains a technically qualified sales staff to solve problems of local users of the products to be sold.

2. Maintains a local inventory of the merchandise the end user needs and will purchase.

3. Extends credit to qualified buyers.

4. Provides transportation of the product from the point of manufacture to the point of use for industrial goods and to the retail outlet for nondurable wholesale goods.

5. Provides service for the product after the sale.

List Price

Many manufacturers sell from a nationally advertised list price. All distributors and many of their customers would know of this price. As the cost of raw materials and market conditions fluctuate a discount from list is given to distributors by the manufacturers and to the end users by the distributor. The discounts vary, but the list price in many industries is seldom changed. Most products with an advertised list price sell to industrial customers at a price discounted from the list.

Selling Price

When merchandise is sold to customers, the price they are charged, if they are paying cash or the amount we invoice them for on a charge sale, is called the selling price. It is determined by subtracting the trade discount (defined later) from the list price.

Selling Price = List Price − Trade Discounts

Net Price

However, many times the customer does not pay the full selling price because a cash discount (defined below) may be offered to encourage customers to pay their bills sooner.

The net price is the selling price minus the allowable discounts such as the cash discount.

Net Price = Selling Price − Allowable Discounts

Note! If no discounts are allowed or taken then the net price and the selling price would be the same.

Net Sale

The net sale is the actual amount of money received by the distributor after all discounts are taken and all adjustments are made. It is not unusual on occasion for adjustments to be made to invoices even after the customer receives the merchandise. Such adjustments could be for substitutions, different quality or specifications from those products originally ordered, goods which are damaged or are unacceptable for whatever reason and for goods returned to the distributor. This is not an exclusive list but gives several examples.

When downward adjustments are made to the amount of the invoice, the customer pays a smaller amount than what was billed on the original invoice. What the customer actually pays represents the net sale. If no discounts are taken and no adjustments are made, then the selling price, the net selling price, and the net sale would all be the same dollar amount.

Cost of Goods Sold (COGS)

The cost of goods sold is the cost of the merchandise to be sold plus any freight charges paid by the wholesaler.

COGS = Cost of Merchandise + Freight

2.2 TERMS OF SALE

As in almost any business transaction where goods are sold and money is exchanged, certain terms or conditions are required by one or more of the parties involved. Distributors generally relate mostly to the terms established by the manufacturers they represent, although distributors may establish terms of sale for their customers also.

Most manufacturers provide a printed sheet for their distributors outlining the "Terms and Conditions" or "General Terms of Sale." This agreement constitutes the generally accepted terms on items sold to the distributor.

A portion of the items commonly found in the terms of sale appear in the following paragraphs and are discussed in a general nature. Consult with specific manufacturers for actual supplier sale terms. Anyone dealing with the acquisition of materials must be completely familiar with the terms of that specific manufacturer (supplier) before an order is placed. An error here can be very expensive.

Freight

The cost to move an item from where it was manufactured to either the distributor's or customer's location is called freight costs.

The terms of sale should specify who is responsible for the payment of freight charges. Large quantities, or high dollar orders, shipped by the least expensive transportation system, are often shipped prepaid (manufacturer pays the freight). Otherwise they may be shipped "prepay and bill" which means the manufacturer paid for the freight, but billed the distributor for what was paid; usually on the same invoice with the bill for the materials.

The term "free on board" (F.O.B.) is commonly used on the invoice to show: 1) who is to pay the transportation charges, 2) who is to control the movement of the shipment, and 3) where the title passes to the buyer. For example, F.O.B. shipping point would mean that the manufacturer would assume the responsibility for putting the merchandise on the truck or rail but all further transportation charges would be paid either by the distributor or the customer. On the other hand, F.O.B.

destination would mean that the manufacturer would put the freight on the carrier and pay to have it delivered to the destination, although unloading would generally still be at the distributor's or customer's expense. Other items may be shipped freight collect (payable by the receiver upon delivery).

If a customer has requested special transportation for which the manufacturer has no allowance, air freight for example, a clear understanding of who is responsible for the charges should be agreed upon between the distributor and the customer before the order is shipped.

Trade Discounts

The trade discount is also a condition or term of the sale and is an amount subtracted by the manufacturer from the manufacturer's suggested list price when the item is sold to the distributor. The trade discounts, discussed in detail in a later chapter, are a means of adjusting the price for variations in the cost of raw materials or competitive pricing in the marketplace. The trade discounts allowed for various volumes or dollar values of orders will ordinarily be outlined in the terms of sale.

Distributors that receive trade discounts may also choose to sell and extend trade discounts to their customers in order to meet local, competitive market conditions.

Cash Discounts

Cash discounts are also outlined in the terms of sale. The cash discount is an amount which can be subtracted or taken from the total amount of the invoice by the purchaser before paying the bill. Cash discounts are offered to encourage early payment of invoices and thus enhance the seller's cash flow.

Special Orders

Special orders usually consist of standard products with slight modification to design, finish, materials, packaging, and etc. When the distributor accepts an order for a special item from a customer the distributor must inform the customer of the supplier's charge for cancellation, usually spelled out in the terms of sale. It is not uncommon for the customer to make a change in the design and cancel a special order. The wholesaler must not be put in the position of having to pay that cancellation charge. In the case mentioned here, this is the responsibility of the customer.

Maximum Charge

Manufacturers who market through distribution expect the distributor to handle small orders. This is one of the services the distributor provides and is the reason that the various trade discounts are given. Because most manufacturer's costs of handling an order are high, they have a high dollar value minimum order size–often $75.00 to $100.00 or more. To place an order for a $25.00 item with a company whose terms of sale include a $75.00 minimum order would be an expensive error. If a customer needed such an item the distributor would try to buy several other items that are needed on the same order to meet the minimum requirement.

Claims

The terms of sale should indicate the time limit, address of contact, and other pertinent information needed in order to make a claim for billing or shipping errors, shortages or other claims. In case of damage the person receiving the freight at the distributorship should clearly write the problem directly on the bill of lading before signing for the shipment. You should also get the delivering agent to sign and date it.

Returns

Also included in the terms should be information concerning how, when and where items may be returned (returnable wire reels for example).

This is not meant to be an exclusive list of terms of sale but cover the basic concepts.

2.3 FINANCIAL TERMS

Several terms are introduced here. You should have a thorough understanding of their relationship to each other. A significant change in any one of these will affect the profitability of the wholesaler.

Cash Flow

Cash flow is the circulation of funds (monies) from cash in the bank into purchased inventory, from sold inventory into accounts receivable, and back into cash in the bank when the customers pay their bills.

The objective is to use as little cash as necessary and circulate it as often as possible each year. If merchandise was purchased and sold within 45 days and the customer paid for the merchandise in another 45 days, the cash flow cycle would have covered 90 days. The shorter the cycle time, the less cash is required to finance the business.

Pricing

The price for which a product sells is generally suggested by the manufacturer. It is the supplier's responsibility to monitor the markets served and know the prices products of their type and quality will sell for in that market. However, since distributors now own the products, the actual selling price is determined by what they are willing to take for the product. This is dependent upon the level of service provided and the availability of competitive products. Ultimately, the competition sets the price of goods in the marketplace.

The distributor will buy the product at list price less a trade discount. The discount provided is how the distributor is paid for the services rendered the manufacturer and the customer. The distributors primary services would include buying, warehousing, selling, providing transportation and servicing the product locally, to mention only a few of the services provided.

Margin

The margin, or gross margin, is a much misunderstood term. It should never be referred to as gross profit or gross profit margin, although these are common terms. Why, because it is neither gross nor profit; it is the margin. The margin is the difference between what the distributor pays for an item and the amount received from its sale.

Margin = Selling Price − COGS − Adjustments

The margin dollars earned on a sale are used to pay employee costs in wages, benefits and all other costs of doing business; and should generate sufficient funds for a reasonable profit.

A common adjustment to the selling price which affects the gross margin is the cash discount. If cash discounts are taken or other adjustments are made to the selling price, then the spendable gross margin dollars would decrease dollar for dollar with the adjustment.

For example, if an item sold for $100.00 and had a cost of goods of $75.00, then the gross margin should be $25.00. However, if a 2% cash discount were offered and taken by the buyer ($100.00 × .02 = $2.00), then $2.00 would be subtracted from the selling price to reach the net price. Since this did not decrease the cost of goods sold, this $2.00 discount would come directly from the gross margin. We would now have only $23.00 in gross margin with which to pay our costs of doing business, not the $25.00 we had calculated in the selling price.

Percent Gross Margin (PGM)

The concept of percent gross margin is common in this industry. The figure represents the relationship between COGS and the selling price expressed as a percent.

$$\text{Percent Gross Margin} = \frac{\text{Selling Price} - \text{COGS}}{\text{Selling Price}} \times 100$$

Markup

It is also true that the gross margin in dollars and the markup in dollars are both the difference between what you paid for an item and what you sold it for.

Markup = Selling Price in dollars − COGS

Percent Markup (PMU)*

The percent markup is commonly used when determining the selling price of an item being priced from the manufacturer's invoice (COGS).

$$\text{Percent Markup} = \frac{\text{Selling Price} - \text{COGS}}{\text{COGS}} \times 100$$

*There is a significant relationship between percent gross margin (PGM) and percent markup (PMU). *If both were transformed into dollars, the amounts would be identical.* However, a word of *caution* is in order. PGM and PMU are *not* calculated in the same manner even though they garner the same dollar result (follow the formulas provided above).

Net Profit

Unless otherwise stipulated, the words "net profit" *as used in this context* will represent the net profit before state or federal income taxes have been imposed, commonly called net profit before taxes (NPBT).

The NPBT represents the money which remains after the cost of goods, all costs of selling, and all operating expenses have been deducted (except state and federal income taxes).

Net Profit After Tax

The net profit after tax (NPAT) represents the money which the owner can spend, distribute among the shareholders or reinvest in the company to insure its growth. If the distributorship has experienced an increase in sales during the current year, the NPAT has generally already been invested in inventory and accounts receivable in order to enhance the growth.

Accounts Payable

This is the money we owe for products we purchased from the manufacturer or for services or products purchased from other local companies.

We generally do not pay cash for these items at the time of purchase but charge them and pay at a later date. Until these bills are paid, this is an *interest-free debt*. If we have to borrow money to pay these bills, then we would begin to pay interest immediately.

Therefore, extending payables legitimately is good business assuming we do not lose a cash discount, damage our credit or lose favor with the company we owe.

Days Receivables or Days Sales Outstanding

This is the money our customers owe us for goods or services we provided to them. Our receivables are usually the only interest-free debt they have. Consequently, many of the distributor's customers will be as slow in paying as our credit policy will permit, thus trying to gain the maximum advantage of the interest-free debt.

Days Receivables or Days Sales Outstanding

Most associations collect data from their members and inform them of the number of days receivables in their industry and local market. Days receivables, also commonly called "days sales outstanding," may be calculated by using the formula shown below.

$$\text{Days Receivables} = \frac{\text{Receivable dollars} \times 365}{\text{Sales}}$$

The author likes the term "days sales outstanding" because it explains what is actually happening in the business. If customers owe your company an amount equal to 45 days receivables this means that you have not been paid for the average of all of the sales you have had in the past 45 days.

Inventory

The distributor's inventory is made up of the items purchased, brought into the warehouse and held on hand for resale to customers. Inventory may also be called stock.

Inventory Turn

When an item is purchased, *put into inventory*, sold, the money collected and another product purchased, we have completed one inventory turn.

$$\text{Inventory Turn} = \frac{\text{Cost of Goods Sold from Inventory}}{\text{Average Warehouse Inventory}}$$

Average Warehouse Inventory

Unfortunately, many wholesalers exaggerate their turn rate because they include drop shipment sales even though the product did not go through the inventory but was delivered directly to the job site. This method makes the turn rate look better, but the resulting figures are erroneous.

Another problem commonly associated with calculating inventory turns is the practice of using the sales figure instead of the cost of goods sold. This also inflates the turn rate. It looks good, but it is untrue.

Inventory Turn and Earn Index

The true inventory turn and earn index is calculated only on sales made from the merchandise held in inventory in the warehouse and correctly uses the cost of goods sold from that inventory.

$$\text{Turn} = \frac{\text{Cost of Goods Sold from Inventory}}{\text{Average Warehouse Inventory}}$$

$$\text{Earn} = \frac{\text{Gross Margin on Sales from Inventory}}{\text{Sales From Inventory}}$$

Inventory Profitability Index = Turn X Earn

This formula is known as the turn and earn profitability index.

Gross Margin Return on Inventory Investment (GMROII)

The GMROII is a better measure of how well the distributor used the inventory to gain margin dollars than is the turn and earn and is therefore a much better measure. The well managed distributor should have a GMROII of $1.50 to $2.00 or more. A GMROII of $1.50 means that for every one dollar invested in inventory last year the distributor earned $1.50 in gross margin dollars. The GMROII is calculated by using the formula

$$\text{GMROII} = \frac{\text{Percent Gross Margin Earned on Warehouse Sales}}{1 - \text{Percent Gross Margin}} \times \text{Inventory Turns}$$

or

$$\text{GMROII} = \frac{\text{Gross Margin Dollars Earned on Warehouse Sales}}{\text{Average Warehouse Inventory}}$$

Summary

The following graph depicts the relationship between some of the major business terms previously discussed. Learn the relationships between the various parts then commit them to memory. (The graphs are not draw proportionately.)

HOW MONEY IS DISTRIBUTED BASED ON MFG'S LIST PRICE

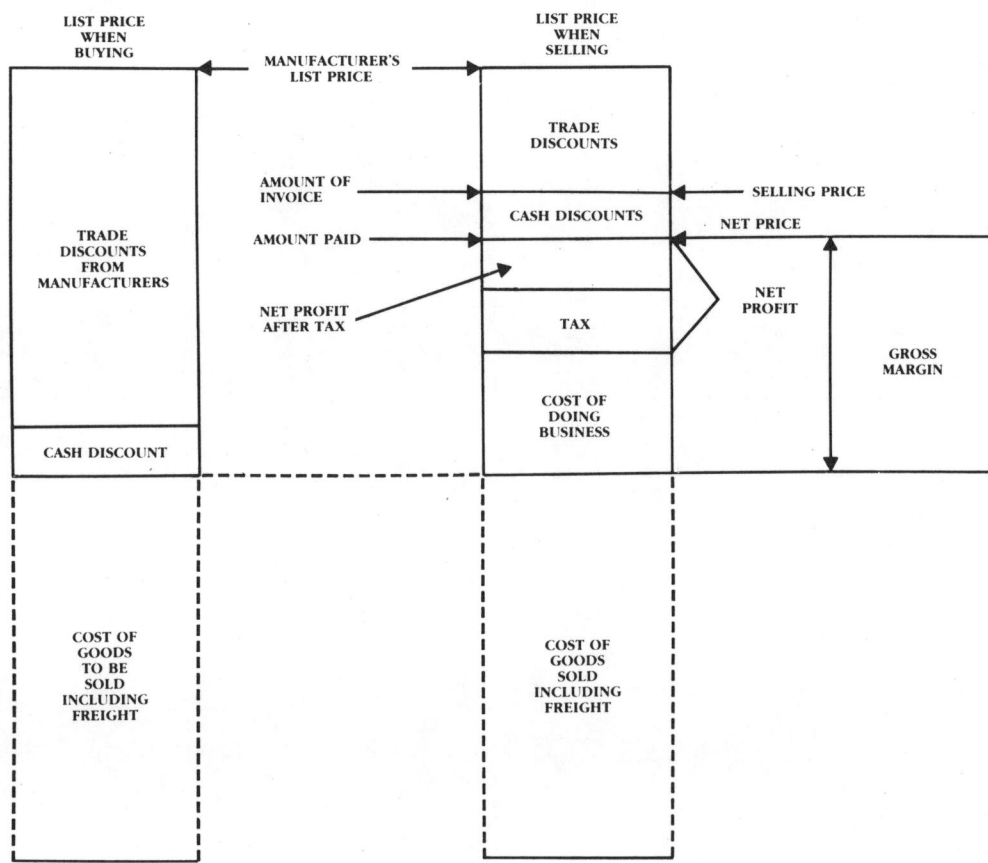

It is very important that you learn quickly and retain permanently the *relationship between the various terms* such as list price, selling price, trade discounts, cash discounts, net price, cost of goods sold, gross margin, and net profit before and after federal and state income taxes. The ability to visualize the relationship between the parts of the sale will enable you to actually draw your own graph to assist you in solving everyday financial word problems in business.

Word problems require an understanding of these business relationships as well as a thorough working knowledge of business mathematics. Although the math is quite simple, complex variables exist which make full understanding of the principles very important to you as you calculate sales, costs and pricing which affect the profitability of your company.

Chapter 3

Percentages in Wholesaling

3.1 CALCULATING THE PERCENT

The most common way of expressing business quantities is to use percentage. Almost all ratios such as profit on sales, discounts, rate of increase or decrease, commission on gross margin and many others are expressed in percentages. Therefore, it is essential to understand the meaning of the terms and formulas used in this method of expression.

Percent means hundredths or "by the hundred." If you consider 100 items in a carton, five of these items would represent 5% or 5 hundredths of the total.

$5 \div 100 = .05 = 5\%$

Terms

Percentage — "P" Percentage is a manner of expressing relationships of hundredths or percents, a common practice in solving business problems.

Rate — "R" The number of hundredths of the base. It should be remembered that the word "rate" is often used for the word "percent."

Base — "B" The number or quantity from which percent is taken. Hint. This is almost always the largest of the three numbers discussed here.

Fractions and Percent Percent is a fraction with 100 as the denominator. Twenty-five percent represents 25/100 and is written 25%. A percent may also be written as a fraction which can then be expressed as a decimal.

$25 \div 100 = 1/4 = .25 = 25\%$

Rules

1. To change a number to percent, multiply the number by 100 (move the decimal two places to the right) and add a percent sign.

   .55 expressed as a percent is

   .55 × 100 = 55%

2. To change a percent to a whole number or decimal fraction, divide the percent by 100 (move the decimal two places to the left and remove the % sign).

   5% = 5 ÷ 100 = .05

Types of Problems

Percentage problems can be expressed in three forms:

1. Computing the percent of a quantity

2. Calculating the rate (or percent)

3. Ascertaining the base

Applying Rule 1: When a percent is more than 100, such as 320%, it means that more than one unit is represented.

320% = 320 ÷ 100 = 3.20 = 3 whole units and .20 of another

Exercises in Calculations

Reduce each of the following common fractions to:

   1) hundredths

   2) decimal form

   3) percent form

(Note: Round all numbers to 4 places right of the decimal before adding the percent sign).

Use this format:

$$1/2 = 50 \div 100 = .5000 = 50\%$$

$$2/3 = .6667 \times 100 = 66.67\%$$

1. 1/5
2. 1/4
3. 1/3
4. 3/7
5. 4/5
6. 7/16
7. 13/21
8. 3/4
9. 11/80
10. 1/12
11. 13/16
12. 5/8
13. 3/10
14. 4/17
15. 9/10

3.2 CALCULATING THE PERCENTAGE

Formula: Percentage = Rate X Base or
P = RB

The percentage is calculated by multiplying the rate by the base. Calculating the percentage is actually finding what number a given percent is of another number.

Example 1

What is 30% of 75?

Since 30% is 30/100 = .30, it is also true, according to the formula, that 30 ÷ 100 X 75 = .30 X 75 = 22.50. Therefore, 30% of 75 is 22.50.

Example 2

A salesperson makes 4% commission on industrial sales. If the net sales for the month were $35,000, how much commission was earned?

P = R X B (or)

Commission = Rate X Net Sales

P = 4% X $35,000

   = 4 ÷ 100 X $35,000

   = .04 X $35,000

   = $1,400 Commission

Exercise I

Calculate the percentage in the following problems:

1. 25% of $1,500
2. 18% of $1,278
3. 11-1/2% of $750
4. 15-2/3% of $2,410
8. 78-1/2% of $696
9. 66-2/3% of $8,760
10. 87-1/8% of $116
11. 1/2% of $500

5. 16% of $8,700
6. 45% of $17,500
7. 90% of $20,380

12. 1/4% of $61
13. 5/8% of $741
14. 15/16% of $15

Exercise II

Calculate the percentage in the following simple statement problems:

1. How much is 35% of 123?
2. What number represents 300% of 444?
3. Find 3/10% of 115.
4. How much is 18% of 40?
5. Find 7% of 49.

Exercise III

Calculate the percentage in the following complex statement problems:

1. A salesperson received 5% commission on sales. If the annual sales were $1,250,000, how much commission was earned?

2. A salesperson receives a 5% commission on sales over $500,000. If the sales were $650,000, how much commission was earned?

3. The machinery and fixtures necessary to equip a plant cost a total of $520,000. If the machinery represented 60% of this total cost, find the cost of each.

4. Ace Distributing Company has $53,000 in inventory. Twenty-three percent are "C" classification items, 32% are class "B" items, and the remainder are class "A" items. What is the value of the "A", "B", and "C" inventory items calculated separately?

5. A. A company's operating expenses average 18% of the net sales. Find the expected amount of expenses if the net sales were $580,000.

   B. Find the amount of expenses that one might expect for net sales of $730,000.

6. A salesperson was paid a salary of $18,000 last year. At the first of this year, an 8% cost-of-living increase was granted. What was the amount of the increase?

7. A company's gross margin represents 21% of its sales. Find the gross margin if the sales for a year are $780,000.

8. ABC Distributors borrowed $86,000 at 8% interest per year. Calculate the amount of interest due for the year.

9. On an investment of $29,000, a distributor makes 27%. If the company incurred expenses equal to 78% of what was made, how much money remained which could be spent by the owner?

3.3 CALCULATING THE RATE

The rate is the number of hundredths of the base. The rate may be calculated by dividing the percentage by the base, using this formula:

R = P ÷ B

Note: Finding the rate is the same as finding what percent one number is of another.

Example 1

A distributor collected accounts receivable of $3,400 and the cost of goods sold was $2,550. The cost of goods represented what percent of the distributor's collections?

R = P ÷ B
   = $2,550 ÷ $3,400
   = .75
   = 75%

Example 2

Twenty-five is what percent of 150? The base is 150 and the percentage is 25. Another way to state this is:

R = P ÷ B
R = 25 ÷ 150
R = 25 ÷ 150 = .1667 × 100 = 16.67%

Example 3

An industrial salesperson received a commission of $75 on net sales of $1,400. What rate of commission did the person make?

R = P ÷ B (or) Rate = $\frac{\text{Commission}}{\text{Net Sales}}$
   = $75 ÷ $1,400
   = .0535 × 100
   = 5.35%

Exercise I

Calculate the rate when the percentage and base are known.

1. _____ % of $8 = 0.79
2. _____ % of .85 = 0.75
3. _____ % of 28 = 18
4. _____ % of 53 = 35
5. _____ % of 1/4 = 12.5
6. _____ % of 1/2 = 0.60
7. _____ % of 9/16 = 0.52
8. _____ % of $75 = $25
9. _____ % of $190 = $85
10. _____ % of $104 = $80
11. _____ % of $223 = $68
12. _____ % of $241 = $30
13. _____ % of $75 = $70
14. _____ % of $150 = $11
15. _____ % of $57 = $46

Exercise II

Calculate the rate of these simple statement problems:

1. 51 is what percent of 85?
2. 23 is what percent of 68?
3. What percent of 52 is 62?
4. What percent of 156 is 270?
5. 4,863 is what percent of 10,816?

Exercise III

Calculate the rate of these complex statement problems:

1. A delivery truck which costs $12,500 is insured for $10,000.
   A. What percent of the risk is assumed by the distributor?
   B. The insurance covers what percent of the cost?

2. A distributor employs 120 men and 67 women.
   A. What percent of the employees are men?
   B. What percent are women?

3. The total production of a western states manufacturer during a recent year was $6,580,000. Product "A" was valued at $1,579,200 and product "B" was valued at $1,217,300.
   A. What percent of the production was product "A"?
   B. What percent of the production was product "B"?

4. A company pays $1,500 on a debt of $2,250.
   A. What percent of the debt do they still owe?
   B. If an additional payment of $250 is made, what percent of the original debt is still owed?

5. A distributor bought a truck for $8,400 and sold it for $3,640 at the end of two years. If the straight line **annual depreciation** rate was 20% of the cost of the truck per year, did they lose by the sale?

3.4 CALCULATING THE BASE

Example 1

A distributor spent $750 last year to repair one truck. This amount was 25% of the total repair expense. Find the total expense.

$B = P \div R$

$= \dfrac{\$750}{.25}$

Total repair = $3,000

Example 2

Twenty percent of a number is equal to 25. Find the number.

$B = P \div R$

$= \dfrac{25}{.20}$

$= 125$

Exercise I

Calculate the base when the percentage and rate are given:

1. 16% of _____ = 64
2. 32% of _____ = 39
3. 29% of _____ = 334
4. 2% of _____ = 8
5. 4% of _____ = 11
6. 9% of _____ = 573
7. 7-1/2% of _____ = 60
8. 9-1/4% of _____ = 27
9. 6-2/3% of _____ = 75
10. 119% of _____ = 97
11. 180% of _____ = 72
12. 219% of _____ = 43
13. 117% of _____ = 19.5
14. 8-1/2% of _____ = 1.5
15. 118% of _____ = 3.05

Exercise II

Calculate the base in these simple statement problems:

1. 40% of what number is 800?
2. 2.5% of what number is 10?
3. 15 is 30% of what number?
4. Forty-five is 8% of what number?
5. Seventy-five is 150% of what number?

Exercise III

Calculate the base when the percentage and rate are given:

1. The operating costs of a distributor were 23% of gross sales. If the costs were $4,991.00, find the gross sales.

2. A distributor paid income tax of $7,012.50 which was 13-3/4% of the annual income. What was the annual income?

3. A distributor's family can pay off a mortgage on their home in 6 years if each year they pay $8,800 which is 16% of their annual income.
   A. How much is their annual income?
   B. Find the amount of the mortgage.

4. A construction contractor bought a saw on sale for 40% off list price. The saw cost $165. What was the list price?

5. The expenses of a distributor last year amounted to $19,895. The amount was 23% of the gross sales.
   A. Find the gross sales.
   B. If the net profit was equal to 6% of the gross sales, find the net profit.

6. A distributor's gross margin for one week was 25% of his sales. If his gross margin was $19,177, what were the sales for the week?

7. A salesperson receives a commission of 16.5% of the gross margin. If the commission is $4,000, what is the gross margin?

8. The operating expenses of a manufacturer last month were $14,342. This amount was 60% of the gross margin. Find the gross margin.

9. A distributor purchases a truck and uses it for one year and sells it for $16,500 which is 12-1/2% less than what he paid for it. Find the value of the truck when it was purchased.

3.5 PERCENT OF CHANGE BETWEEN NUMBERS

It is common practice in business to discuss the difference between two corresponding numbers as "percent increase" or "percent decrease."

The *percent increase* is used when a number becomes larger (increases) over a period of time.

The *percent decrease* is used when a number becomes smaller (decreases) over a period of time.

Example 1

A salesperson earned a commission of $22,000 last year. This year the commission was $24,500. Find the percent increase from one year to the next.

First, find the amount of change:

$24,500 − $22,000 = $2,500 Increase

Formula: R = P ÷ B

$$= \frac{\$2{,}500}{\$22{,}000}$$

$$= 11.36\% \text{ Increase}$$

The $22,000 represents the base because this is the number of which we are seeking the percent increase. The $2,500 is the percentage increase. The rate of increase is 11.36% (percent and rate being the same).

Example 2

Corporate earnings in the previous quarter were $382,000. However, during the present quarter, earnings decreased to $360,000. Find the rate (percent) of the decrease.

First, find the amount of change:

$382,000 − $360,000 = $22,000 Decrease

Formula: R = P ÷ B

$$= \frac{\$22,000}{\$382,000}$$

$$= 5.76\%$$

The figure $382,000 is used because this is the number which was decreased by the rate being sought.

The concept of the percent change per year over multiple periods of time is often used in business.

Example 3

A business is projected by the management to grow 8% per year for the next five years. Their present sales volume is 1.5 million dollars.

Find their projected sales volume the fifth year: $1.5 million is the base number to be increased. Find the percentage increase:

P = B × R

= $1.5 million × .08

= $120,000 increase the first year

The $120,000 must now be added to the $1.5 million to find the projected sales volume at the end of the first year.

$1,500,000 + $120,000 = $1,620,000

The amount $1,620,000 is now used to calculate the sales volume for the second year, using the same formula as in the first step. This is repeated until the fifth-year figure is ascertained. However, when using your computer or electronic calculator there is a much simpler method which achieves the same result.

Example 3 (Simplified)

The desired number which represented sales at the end of the first year was ascertained by multiplying the base by the rate and adding this number to the base. This is represented in the formula which follows:

($1,500,000 × .08) + $1,500,000 = $1,620,000

The same result can be achieved by a simpler method, i.e.,

$1,500,000 × 1.08 = $1,620,000

Note! The figure "1" in the multiplication formula simply replaces the need for the addition step because this figure represents that same number.

By entering the number $1,500,000 into the calculator and multiplying by 1.08 five consecutive times, we get the desired figure for the fifth year.

$1,500,000 × 1.08 × 1.08 × 1.08 × 1.08 × 1.08 = $2,203,992 (See Complete Below)

	Sales
$1,500,000 × 1.08 = $1,620,000	1st Year
$1,620,000 × 1.08 = $1,749,600	2nd Year
$1,749,600 × 1.08 = $1,889,568	3rd Year
$1,889,568 × 1.08 = $2,040,733	4th Year
$2,040,733 × 1.08 = $2,203,992	5th Year

The percent decrease is calculated by much the same method used when the decrease occurs over an extended period of time and the decrease is to be *calculated* on the *declining balance*.

Example 4

A distributor's new building cost $172,500. Find its value at the end of the third year if it depreciated at the rate of 4% on the declining value each year.

Depreciation the 1st year = Cost × Rate = $172,500 × .04 = $6,900

Value at end of first year = $172,500 − $6,900 = $165,600

Depreciation second year = $165,600 × .04 = $6,624

Value at end of second year = $165,600 − $6,624 = $158,976

Depreciation third year = $158,976 × .04 = $6,359

Value at end of third year = $158,976 − $6,359 = $152,617

Example 4 (Simplified)

The same result can be achieved in fewer steps by using a multiplier factor. In the previous example, the base ($172,500) was multiplied by the rate (4%) and the percentage subtracted from the base to find the value at the end of each period.

However, if 100% is equal to $172,500, then 96% (100% − 4%) is equal to the new number after the decrease. This can be entered readily into the calculator, reducing the chance for error. Thus, we solve the above problem as follows:

100% − 4% = 96%

$172,500 × .96 × .96 × .96 = Value at end of the third year

$172,500 × .96 = $165,600
$165,600 × .96 = $158,976
$158,976 × .96 = $152,617
(Rounded to whole dollars)

Exercise I

Calculate the percent change in these simple statement problems:

1. A distributor's inventory increased from 1,200 items to 1,400 items. What was the percent increase?

2. A motorized cable rack was valued at $81,000. It decreased in value to $70,000. What was the percent decrease?

3. During the fall and spring, a distributor made 120 deliveries per day. In the summer, the deliveries increased to 180 per day. Find the percent increase in deliveries.

4. A compressor which cost $695 new was declared obsolete and sold for $400. What was the percent decrease in the value of the compressor?

Exercise II

1. The sales of a distributor increased 15% per year for five years. If the sales were $28,965 at the end of the first year, find the sales for the fifth year.

2. The sales of a manufacturer's representative increased 8% each year for four years. If the sales the first year amounted to $23,685, find the sales for the fourth year.

3. A salesperson had weekly sales of $40,000. She accepted a new product line and increased her sales 2%, 8%, and 12% respectively for the next three weeks. What were her sales at the end of the third week?

4. A distributor depreciated a piece of machinery by the declining balance method 50% the first year, 25% the second year, and 8% for two remaining years. If the machine cost $9,500 when purchased, what was the depreciated value at the end of the fourth year?

5. A manufacturer's sales of $69,578 increased 8% per year for three years, declined by 12% for one year and then increased by 4% for three years. What were the sales for the seventh year?

Example:

A distributor received a shipment of 384 boxes of bolts which were sold at the following rates: 18-3/4% at $2.45 per box, and 50% of the "remainder" at $1.80 per box. Of the parts still remaining unsold, 25% were damaged and the balance was sold at $1.15 per box.

Find the total amount received.

Find the percent of the total sale of each separate sale.

Total boxes of parts = 384 = 100%

384 X 18.75% =
72 boxes X $2.45 = $176.40

384-72 = (312 X .50)
156 boxes X $1.80   = $280.80

156 X .25 Damaged   = 39

156 – 39 = 117 boxes X $1.15 = $134.55

Total Sale   = $591.75

$\dfrac{\$176.40}{\$591.75}$ = 29.81% were sold at $2.45

$\dfrac{\$280.80}{\$591.75}$ = 47.45% were sold at $1.80

$\dfrac{\$134.55}{\$591.75}$ = 22.74% were sold at $1.15

$591.75 = 100% of those sold.

Exercise III

1. A distributor received a shipment of 540 tons of tumbling abrasive which was sold at the following rates: 25 tons at $2,450 per ton and 50% of the remainder at $1,800 per ton. Twenty-five percent of the balance which remained was sold for $1,150 per ton.

   Find the total amount of money the distributor received.

   What percentage of the total tonnage was unsold?

2. Salespeople with ABC Distributors received commission on a graduated basis. Their top salesperson sold $51,000 of "A" classification products for which she received 1.5% commission; she sold $17,500 of "B" classification products for which she received 2% commission; and she sold $5,000 of "C" classification products for which she received 3% commission. What was her total commission for the month?

3. How much commission would a salesperson make with the compensation method in Question 2 with sales of $47,500, $15,000, and $3,500 on classification "A" "B", and "C" items respectively?

4. A distributor received a shipment of 84 tons of reinforcing bar which sold at the following rates: 60% at $1,750 per ton and 75% of the remainder at $1,400 per ton. The unsold portion had been damaged in shipment and was sold at $900 per ton. What was the total amount of money received?

5. A salesperson had received orders for $75,000 per month on which she earned a commission of two percent. However, the actual billings by the company were only $60,250, not the full $75,000. What difference in dollars did this make in her commission check?

6. A distributor had $300,000 in sales during his first year in business; 35% of this was from abrasives and 10% from hand tools. Of the remainder, 75% was represented by electrical goods and the balance from general maintenance equipment. What was the dollar value of each?

7. A distributor received 240 carbide-tipped circular saw blades at a special rate from the manufacturer. The company sold 47.9% of these at $95 each, 64% of the remainder at $83.50 each, and the others at $67.50 each. What was the total dollar amount received?

8. A distributor received a shipment of 27,000 feet of rubber hydraulic hose which he sold at the following rates: 42% at $12 per foot, 10% at $9.95 per foot, and 60% of the remainder at $8.95 per foot.

   What was the total dollar amount received?

   What percent was unsold?

9. A distributor made $105,000 gross margin last month. Of that amount, 27% went to cover fixed expenses, and 60% covered the variable expenses for the month. How much money did

the distributor have left after expenses?

10. A distributor had in stock 17,000 pounds of connectors which he decided to discontinue. The company sold 65% the first month at $2.95 per pound, and 10% the next month at $2.15 per pound. The remainder, now obsolete, was valued at $1.44 per pound and deducted as a loss from taxable income.

   Find the total amount of money the distributor received.

   What was the dollar value of the loss?

   What percent of the total income did the loss represent?

11. A salesperson working on salary plus commission receives a salary of $18,000 per year. The commission is 3% of his gross margin over $180,000. He also receives a $600 bonus if his gross margins for the year are $240,000 or more. What is his annual salary if the gross margin is $250,000?

12. A tool set sells for the list price of $380. If the distributor makes 22% gross margin on the sale, how much did the tool set cost the distributor?

13. Ace Distributing Company had an inventory of $364,000. They had it insured for 75% of full value at a rate of $.80 per $100. What was their annual premium?

14. A distributor is overstocked on one inventory item. In order to turn the inventory, he sells the merchandise at a loss of 50% of the cost of the goods. The loss is equal to what percent of the selling price?

Chapter 4

Trade Discounts

4.1 TRADE DISCOUNTS

In order to maximize the small profits which the wholesaler makes, all employees need to thoroughly understand how to apply Trade Discounts. Manufacturers providing trade discounts to their wholesale partners is a common practice in industry today. Trade discounts serve many useful purposes (which will be discussed), but the scope of the discounts is often misunderstood by new people entering the wholesaling industry, as well as some who have been in it for some time. Because they fail to understand the relationship of discounts to gross margin, some give trade discounts which are devastating to the margin of the wholesaler. For example, if a product is usually sold at a gross margin of 25%, to give a discount of 10% off the customary selling price is to give away 40% of the gross margin ($.10 \div .25 = .40 = 40\%$)! This is disastrous, yet many do it. Let's work through several examples to see the purpose and effect of trade discounts.

A trade discount is an amount subtracted by the manufacturer from the suggested list price of an item when it is sold to the distributor for resale. This determines the amount to be paid by the wholesaler. Even though many products are not sold from list price less discounts, those manufacturers who do publish and distribute list prices do so in order to establish one common price which will prevail nationally. The discounts (deductions) are usually expressed as a percent of the list price.

For example, a wholesaler purchases fittings from the manufacturer for resale to industrial or contractor customers. The manufacturer's suggested list price (nationally advertised) for this particular item is $3.00 each. The manufacturer packages the items 100 in a standard package, allows the wholesaler a 45% trade discount from the list price and prepays the freight. What is the invoice price or the price paid by the wholesaler?

Invoice Price = List Price − Trade Discount

List Price = $3.00 X 100 items

= $300.00

Invoice Price = $300.00 − ($300 X .45)

= $300.00 − $135.00

Invoice Price = $165.00

The wholesaler's cost for each item would be the same as the invoice price divided by 100 or $1.65 each.

This is simple enough, but the cost of labor, capital and raw material is not stable in some market segments, especially where copper, silver and other semiprecious or precious metals are used, as in the electrical and electronic industries. Therefore, if a manufacturer publishes a catalog or price sheet (for one of these industries) in which prices are quoted, the prices must be high enough so a substantial discount can be allowed. When the selling price needs to be changed due to changing costs, only the discount from list need be altered. This concept prevents the printed material from becoming obsolete on the first price change. In industries where list prices are rarely changed, the wholesaler's cost of goods is kept current with changing costs by altering only the percentage of the discount.

Since the manufacturer's suggested list price is often an advertised price and since most wholesalers also offer a trade discount to their customers, the trade discounts are often "multiple or chain discounts." A multiple discount is a series of two or more discounts taken in succession. The first discount is called the lead discount while subsequent discounts are called supplementary discounts.

For example, a manufacturer of copper wire has experienced a downward fluctuation in the price of copper, thus lowering the cost of copper wire to the wholesaler. The manufacturer passes this price reduction on to the wholesaler in the form of a second or possibly third, fourth or fifth trade discount. Recently, a certain wire size and type carried a trade discount of 25%. With the reduction in the cost of copper, the discount became 25% and 10%. An additional 5% was offered for orders larger than a specified dollar value.

In the industry, this series of discounts is read as "twenty-five, ten, and five." The discounts are taken successively as shown below on the purchase of 20 rolls of wire:

Step 1. List price of the wire = $100 (per roll)
Invoice = $100 × 20 = $2,000
The first discount of 25% is:
$2,000 × .25 = $500

Step 2. Deduct the amount of the discount from the list price:
$2,000 − $500 = $1,500

Step 3. Find the second discount (10%) from the previously discounted price:
$1,500 × .10 = $150

Step 4. Subtract this from the previously discounted price:
$1,500 − $150 = $1,350

Because the wholesaler purchased a sufficient quantity, an additional trade discount of 5% was also allowed.

Step 5. Find the quantity discount:
$1,350 × .05 = $67.50

Step 6. Subtract this discount from the previous price to find the invoice price:
$1,350 − $67.50 = $1,282.50
Invoice for 20 rolls = $1,282.50

IT IS IMPORTANT THAT THE READER BE AWARE THAT CHANGING THE ORDER OF THE DISCOUNTS DOES NOT CHANGE THE END RESULTS. To check, run the numbers through your calculator to see that you get the same answer.

Although the method shown above does help one understand what is happening with trade discounts, and it does achieve the desired result, it is very laborious and the various steps take time to perform, thus increasing the probability of error.

4.2 SIMPLIFIED METHOD

A simplified method of calculating the amount to be paid by the wholesaler is available and lends itself readily to electronic calculator and computer applications.

In this simplified calculation, the list price is 100%. The percent discount is subtracted from 100% and the percentage multiplier calculated in your head. In the previous example, the trade discounts were 25%, 10% and 5%. The price paid by the wholesaler is calculated as follows:

Formula 1

Lead discount = 25%

100% − 25% = 75% or .75
where .75 is the multiplier

75% of $2,000 = .75 X $2,000

= $1,500

The trade discount of 25% had an equivalent multiplier of .75. In every case, the discount and its corresponding *multiplier* added together equal (.25 + .75) = 1.0. You have no doubt noticed that when we multiply a number by a fraction, the product is smaller, thus providing the discount without the subtraction step. The second discount was 10%.

$1,500 = 100%

Discount = 10%

100% -10% = 90% or .90 multiplier

90% of $1,500 = .90 X $1,500

= $1,350

The third discount was 5%.

$1,350 = 100%

100% − 5%   = 95%

95% of $1,350   = .95 × $1,350

Invoice Amount = $1,282.50

Even though this is the correct method, most electronic calculators allow the calculations to be made in a few simple steps as follows:

Read the discounts of 25%, 10% and 5% and mentally calculate the multipliers by subtracting the percent discount in each case from 100%. The formula then becomes $2,000 × .75 × .90 × .95 = $1,282.50.

No numbers need to be written down except the invoice amount because the result of each step is held in the calculator. The calculation is also much more accurate since most calculators will carry numbers to 8 or more places.

Exercise I

Find the invoice price of the following items and the dollar amount of the discount:

Item	List Price	Lead Disc. %	Second Disc. %	Invoice Amount	Discount Allowed (In $)
1.	$ 20	10		$18.00	$ 2.00
2.	40	9			
3.	93	15			
4.	61	29			
5.	973	16-1/2			
6.	127	8-1/4			
7.	213	28-3/4			
8.	55	10	10	$44.55	$10.45
9.	584	12	8		
10.	323	33	6		
11.	270	14	1		
12.	330	5	1/2		
13.	818	50	5		
14.	439	2-1/2	2-1/4		
15.	91	3-1/2	1/2		

4.3 MULTIPLE DISCOUNTS: USING MULTIPLYING FACTORS

Numbers may be multiplied in any order and achieve the same result. It is also true that if a number is to be multiplied by several other numbers, multiplying the multipliers together first does not change the answer.

Example:

List Price   = $2,000

Discounts   = 25%, 10% and 5%

The multipliers as shown earlier are .75, .90 and .95. In order to calculate a one step multiplier, simply multiply as follows:

.75 X .90 X .95 = .64125

The one step multiplier is .64125.

Apply the one step multiplier:

$2,000 X .64125 = $1,282.50

Check:

$2,000 X .75 X .90 X .95 = $1,282.50

It should be noted that this does not give the amount of the discount, but directly calculates the amount of the invoice, or amount paid by the wholesaler. The amount of the discount can be quickly calculated if it is needed by subtracting the invoice amount from the list price. The dollar amount of the discount is:

$2,000 − $1,282.50 = $717.50

Exercise II

Calculate and record single unit multipliers, invoice amounts and trade discounts received in the problems given below.

Item	List Price		Trade Discounts		Multi-plying	Inv. Amt.	Disc. Recd.
1.	$ 50	20	5	5	.7220	$36.10	$13.90
2.	$ 75	10	5	5			
3.	$ 100	12	6	3			
4.	$1,536	11	2	1/2			
5.	$2,559	5	3	2/3			
6.	$6,243	18	8	7			
7.	$3,818	30	20	1			
8.	$ 120	2.5	2.5	1			
9.	$ 564	40	4	4			
10.	$7,972	50	5	2-1/2			

4.4 TABLE OF MULTIPLIER FACTORS

Below is a list of discount percentages which appear in a standard published table of multiplying factors.

DISCOUNT PERCENTAGES
TABLE OF MULTIPLYING FACTORS

Supple-mentary LEAD	0	2½	5	5 & 2½	TWO FIVES	TWO 5's & 2½	THREE FIVES	THREE 5's & 2½
	A	= A x .975	= A x .95	= A x .92625	= A x .9025	= A x .879938	= A x .857375	= A x .835941
0	1.00	.9750	.9500	.9263	.9025	.8799	.8574	.8359
10	.90	.8775	.8550	.8336	.8123	.7919	.7716	.7523
11	.89	.8678	.8455	.8244	.8032	.7831	.7631	.7440
12	.88	.8580	.8360	.8151	.7942	.7743	.7545	.7356
13	.87	.8440	.8265	.8058	.7852	.7655	.7459	.7273
14	.86	.8385	.8170	.7966	.7762	.7567	.7373	.7189
15	.85	.8288	.8075	.7873	.7671	.7479	.7288	.7105
16	.84	.8190	.7980	.7781	.7531	.7391	.7202	.7022
17	.83	.8093	.7885	.7688	.7491	.7303	.7116	.6938
18	.82	.7995	.7790	.7595	.7401	.7215	.7030	.6855
19	.81	.7898	.7695	.7503	.7310	.7127	.6945	.6771
20	.80	.7800	.7600	.7410	.7220	.7040	.6859	.6688
21	.79	.7703	.7505	.7317	.7130	.6952	.6773	.6604
22	.78	.7605	.7410	.7225	.7040	.6864	.6688	.6520
23	.77	.7508	.7315	.7132	.6949	.6776	.6602	.6437
24	.76	.7410	.7220	.7040	.6859	.6688	.6516	.6353
25	.75	.7313	.7125	.6947	.6769	.6600	.6430	.6270
26	.74	.7215	.7030	.6854	.6679	.6512	.6345	.6186
27	.73	.7118	.6935	.6762	.6588	.6424	.6259	.6102
28	.72	.7020	.6840	.6669	.6498	.6336	.6173	.6019
29	.71	.6923	.6745	.6576	.6408	.6248	.6087	.5935
30	.70	.6825	.6650	.6484	.6318	.6160	.6002	.5852
31	.69	.6728	.6555	.6391	.6227	.6072	.5916	.5768
32	.68	.6630	.6460	.6299	.6137	.5984	.5830	.5684
33	.67	.6533	.6365	.6206	.6047	.5896	.5744	.5601
34	.66	.6435	.6270	.6113	.5957	.5808	.5659	.5517
35	.65	.6338	.6175	.6021	.5866	.5720	.5573	.5434
36	.64	.6240	.6080	.5928	.5776	.5632	.5487	.5350
37	.63	.6143	.5985	.5835	.5686	.5544	.5401	.5266
38	.62	.6045	.5890	.5743	.5596	.5456	.5316	.5183
39	.61	.5948	.5795	.5650	.5505	.5368	.5230	.5099
40	.60	.5850	.5700	.5558	.5415	.5280	.5144	.5016
41	.59	.5753	.5605	.5465	.5325	.5192	.5059	.4932
42	.58	.5655	.5510	.5372	.5235	.5104	.4973	.4848
43	.57	.5558	.5415	.5280	.5144	.5016	.4887	.4765
44	.56	.5460	.5320	.5187	.5054	.4928	.4801	.4681
45	.55	.5363	.5225	.5094	.4964	.4840	.4716	.4598
46	.54	.5265	.5130	.5002	.4874	.4752	.4630	.4514
47	.53	.5168	.5035	.4909	.4783	.4664	.4544	.4430
48	.52	.5070	.4940	.4817	.4693	.4576	.4458	.4347
49	.51	.4973	.4845	.4724	.4603	.4488	.4373	.4263

Sheets of this type are commonly provided to wholesalers by their manufacturers. The sheet illustrated is only one of an infinite number of sheets with a variety of lead and supplementary discounts being possible.

Example

Using the Table of Multiplier Factors, a manufacturer offers the wholesaler trade discounts of 25%, 5% and 5% on purchases on $1,500 worth of tools. The calculations using the simplified method would be as follows:

$1,500 X .75 X .95 X .95 = $1,015.31 (invoice price)

However, the single multiplier factor is

.75 X .95 X .95 = .67687

and applying the factor yields the same result:

$1,500 X .6769 = $1,015.31

When many calculations are being made and the discounts cannot be done mentally, the discount multipliers can be located in the proper table, or you can make up your own multiplier table by using the formula shown above.

Look down the left column entitled "Lead Discount" until you find the lead discount offered, in this case 25%. Then move horizontally across the page until you are directly under the supplementary discount column of "Two Fives." At the intersection of these two lines, you will find the multiplying factor .6769. This factor represents the multiplier to use when calculating the amount of an invoice when the trade discounts are twenty-five and two fives. Most people can learn to use a multiplier table such as this in a matter of minutes. However, it is important to those who will manage others to understand how the tables were created. There is an old but often true statement which says "Those that **know how** may have a job but it is likely that the one that **knows why** will always be their boss." (Author Unknown.)

As mentioned earlier, when the selling price needs to be changed to meet market conditions or reflect changing costs, only the discount from the list price needs to be altered. Changes in the discount rates can usually be accomplished by a single flier or similar printed statement which prevents the previous printed materials from becoming obsolete at the first price change. Therefore, in those industries where list prices are rarely changed, the wholesaler's costs are kept current with market trends by varying the discount.

It is not uncommon for the discount on some products sold to the wholesaler to be 50% of the suggested resale price. Keep in mind that very few products actually sell at list price because competition forces the price down, but the discount structure is a valuable tool to help keep prices in line with market conditions in those industries.

Exercise I

Calculate for each of the following problems: 1. The amount of the invoice 2. The amount of the discount. 3. The multiplying factor.

1. The catalog price of a hand tool is $4.00. This price is subject to discounts of 15-1/2% and 10%.

2. A quantity of merchandise was purchased by a distributor; the list price was $460 less discounts of 16% and 14%.

3. Structural steel materials are advertised at $3,400 per 100 feet. The distributor purchased 10,000 feet and received trade discounts of 22% and 17%, plus quantity discounts of 2-1/2% and 2-1/2%.

4. A carload of conduit was purchased by an electrical distributor at a list price of $86,500. He received trade discounts of 25%, 5%, 1%, and 1/2%.

5. A distributor purchased motor starters listed at $1,500 subject to discounts of 30%, 8% and 3-1/8%, and heaters for the starters, listed at $180, with discounts of 25%, 4-1/4%, and 1-3/4%. (Omit the multiplying factor).

Exercise II

1. A pallet of bar stock was purchased by a distributor. The list price was $460 less discounts of 26% and 14-1/4%. The

goods were sold at the same list price with discounts of 18% and 7%. Find the gross margin or loss on the sale.

2. A distributor bought 12 cases of merchandise which listed at $18.50 each, subject to discounts of 21% and 11%. If the total freight cost was $22.50, how much did each case of goods cost?

3. Which is better and how much better for the distributor who is buying a bill of goods amounting to $360 — a discount of 25%, 20%, and 5%, or a discount of 40% and 10%?

4. An electric drill which listed for $128 is sold to a distributor for $96. What is the rate of the trade discount?

5. A machinist's vise listed at $179, subject to a 25% discount, sells for $120. What additional rate of trade discount was received?

6. A manufacturer of impact tools offered a trade discount of 25% and 20% to the distributors on tools which listed for $245.00. At a pre-inventory sale, an additional discount was offered in order to sell these tools at $122.50. Find the additional percent of the discount offered.

7. Show your work in order to prove that a series of discounts, 20%, 15%, and 5%, is equal to a series of discounts of 15%, 5%, and 20%.

8. A distributor purchased 18 cases of lubricant listed at $24.95 per case of 24 tubes. The sale was subject to discounts of 18%, 9%, and 3-1/2%. Show your work to indicate that the discount per case and the discount per tube are proportional.

9. A distributor can buy electric motors listed at $218.00 each at the following discounts:
1—9 units — 30%,
10 — 15 units — 30% and 10%
A customer requests 9 of these motors on a single order.

Should the distributor purchase nine or ten motors?

Why?

What is the deciding factor?

10. A manufacturer's list price of carbon steel pipe is $56 per linear foot, subject to trade discounts of 25%, 10%, 5%, and 5%. If the distributor purchases 8,900 feet
   1) What is the invoice price per foot?
   2) What is the dollar amount of the discount on the total invoice?
   3) What percent of the list price does the discount represent?

4.5 PAYMENT FOR SERVICES RENDERED

Trade discounts are also extended by manufacturers to their wholesalers as a means of payment to their wholesaler partners for the sales and inventory functions they provide to the manufacturer, as well as to the end user or customer. For example, wholesalers provide a local inventory of merchandise which makes products readily available to the customers. This saves the manufacturer from having to provide that inventory through owning and operating a warehouse in every major market area served. This cost of providing the warehouse and stocking it with inventory is returned to the wholesaler in the form of the trade discount which turns into gross margin dollars when the product is sold (Gross Margin = Selling Price − Cost of Goods Sold).

The same is true of payment for all the other functions the wholesaler provides, which includes product expertise provided by the sales force to customers and the extension of credit to the customers for their convenience of purchasing and payment. In addition, the local wholesaler will usually provide transportation of the products from where they are stored locally to the customer's warehouse or sometimes directly to the point of use. Service after the sale alone justifies a trade discount in order to pay the local wholesaler for time and effort spent in warranty or other customer-satisfying activities on behalf of the manufacturer.

The discussion here lends itself to the thought that the wholesaler makes a good gross margin when the trade discounts are 25%, 5% and 5%. However, make no mistake, the wholesaler makes a very small profit even though the product was bought at a low price. The reason is that the price was low because the demand for the product was low and the supply large. When demand is down and products are in great supply, the law of supply and demand works and prices fall. Because of the sales pressure from the competition, the wholesaler must pass the majority of the savings on to the customer. The trade discount earned is often passed on to the customer by the wholesaler by providing the buyer a discount from the same list price.

For example, a wholesaler purchased from a manufacturer materials with a list price of $2,000 with trade discounts of 25%, 10% and 5%. The actual product cost to the wholesaler was

$2,000 × .75 × .90 × .95 = $1,282.50. However, because of the competitiveness of the market place, the product cannot be sold for list price, but must be sold to the wholesaler's customer at a discount from the list also.

The wholesaler sells the item to a customer at list price subject to trade discount of 15% and 10%. Thus the customer is invoiced for $2,000 × .85 × .90 = $1,530.00. The wholesaler's gross margin on the sale was $247.00. This amounts to only a 16% gross margin, which is small for an out of warehouse sale, but not uncommon in some commodity industries. The percent gross margin is calculated by this formula:

$$\frac{\text{Selling Price} - \text{Cost}}{\text{Selling Price}} = \text{PGM}$$

PGM = Percent Gross Margin

so

$$\frac{\$1,530 - \$1,282}{\$1,530} = .16 \text{ PGM}$$

or 16% Gross Margin

This sale is not disastrous; in fact, well managed wholesalers who sell primarily commodities are being marginally sustained in business at this margin. What is tragic is what happens many times to persons who do not understand the implications of an additional discount.

For example, let's suppose we have already extended to this customer discounts of 15% and 10%. It is not uncommon for that customer to ask (and some wholesaler personnel to give) an additional 5% discount. Purchasing managers are taught to ask for another five. However, we should not give the five, at least not without much consideration. Let's see why.

4.6 PROFIT ERODED BY ADDITIONAL DISCOUNTS

We ordered merchandise with a list price of $2,000 with discounts of 25%, 10% and 5%. We paid $2,000 X .75 X .90 X .95 = $1,282.50. We offer the product for sale to a customer for $2,000 X .85 X .90 = $1,530.00. The customer asks for another 5%. Let's look at the additional discount and see what it does to our profitability. The new discount structure would be $2,000 X .85 X .90 X .95 = $1,453.50 as the new selling price.

By giving the extra five percent, we lowered the selling price from $1,530 to $1,453.50. You need to realize that the gross margin was only ($1,530 − $1,282.50) = $247.50 before the additional discount. The added discount of 5% at this point amounted to $76.50 which is a staggering 31% percent of the 16% gross margin we were trying to make.

The percentage decrease in the gross margin is calculated by subtracting the lower gross margin from the original gross margin before the last discount and dividing by the original gross margin. Thus:

$$\frac{\$247.50 - \$171.00}{\$247.50} = \frac{\$76.50}{\$247.50} = .31$$

or 31% decrease in gross margin.

Giving the customer another 5% off the list price at this point is equal to giving away 31% of the gross margin.

Let's look at another example. A product is purchased for $75.00 and should be sold at a trade price of $100.00. A customer calls and asks for a trade discount of 10%. The product carried a gross margin of 25% if sold at $100.00.

Selling Price − Cost of Goods = Gross Margin

$100.00 − $75.00 = $25.00

$$\text{Percent Gross Margin} = \frac{100 - 75}{100} = .25 \text{ or } (25\%)$$

However, because we gave a 10 percent trade discount, the selling price is now $90.00 ($100.00 X .90 = $90.00).

Gross Margin = $90.00 − $75.00 = $15.00

Percent Gross Margin = $\frac{\$90.00 - \$75.00}{\$90.00}$ = 16.67%

By approving the additional 10% discount, we gave away $10.00 of the $25.00 we should have made. This $10.00 is 40% of the gross margin. The percent change in numbers shows that

$\frac{\$25.00 - \$15.00}{\$25}$ = $\frac{\$10}{\$25}$ = 40% reduction in gross margin

Proof: $25.00 X 40% = $25.00 X .40 = $10.00

Thus the $10.00 (10%) discount was a full 40% of the gross margin.

Think before you act. Calculate before you give any additional discounts. The author has been in wholesale houses where the inside sales force had the authority to give away fives like they were popcorn. In a low gross margin business like the one wholesalers are in, you must be careful not to give away the store. Five percent and 10% discounts do not sound like much, but 5% of the selling price is 31% of the gross margin on a sale with only a 16% margin. A 10% discount is equal to 40% of the gross margin when the gross margin was only 25%. Know your distributor math and do not give away the store.

Chapter 5

Cash Discounts

5.1 GENERAL CASH DISCOUNT TERMINOLOGY

In the previous chapter, we reviewed trade discounts and indicated this was an amount subtracted from the manufacturer's suggested list price when an item was purchased for resale by the wholesaler. We stated this was the manufacturer's means of paying the wholesaler for warehousing the product in the local market, selling the product to the consumer, providing transportation to the contractors or end user, extending credit to the customer and servicing the product after the sale. We also explained this may be a single discount or it may be a series of discounts by which we arrive at the final cost to the wholesaler. However, trade discounts are not the only discounts available to wholesalers.

In this chapter, we will discuss the fact that trade discounts, as well as cash discounts, may be made available to wholesalers by their manufacturers. A cash discount is an amount which can be subtracted or "taken" from the total amount of the invoice by the wholesaler before paying the bill. Cash discounts are offered to wholesalers as encouragement for them to pay their invoices (debts) within a specified period of time, usually considerably shorter than the industry average. The rate of the cash discount allowed is also shown on the invoice. This rate can be taken if the invoice is paid in cash, by check or by electronic funds transfer within the specified time. For example, a two percent cash discount may be offered if an invoice is paid within fifteen days rather than waiting thirty, forty-five days or longer.

It is important to understand that cash discounts are NOT GIVEN. They are OFFERED, then TAKEN or REFUSED by the purchaser. If the cash discount is taken, in this case two percent, this amount may be subtracted from the amount of the invoice and the payment made for the lesser amount. For example, a wholesaler is invoiced for $18,000 and offered a cash discount of two percent if the invoice is paid by the 10th of the following month. The cash discount would be $18,000 × .02 = $360. The amount to be paid is $18,000 × .98 = $17,640. This is a significant amount to be saved simply by paying 20 days sooner.

A two percent cash discount is offered and shown on the face (front) of the invoice in the example given below. Look for the cash discount statement under "Terms."

SAMPLE INVOICE

```
VENDOR:    Basic Manufacturing Co.           INVOICE NO.:   67890
SOLD TO:   Dependable Plumbing Supply Co.    PAGE:          1
           12345 Main Street                 INVOICE DATE:
           Anywhere, U.S.A.  00000
SHIP TO:   Same
```

QTY SHIPPED	ITEM NO./DESCRIPTION	UNIT PRICE	UOM	NET PRICE
1	1 1/4" x 150' GAS POLY PIPE	$63.00	EA.	$63.00
6	BLACK 1 1/4" 90 ELL	1.35	EA.	7.98
4	BLACK 1 1/4" x 1" 90 ELL	1.52	EA.	6.08
1	BLACK 3/4" x 3" NIPPLE	.29	EA.	.29
1	BLACK 1" x 3" NIPPLE	.39	EA.	.39
6	BLACK 1 1/4" x CLOSE NIPPLE	.39	EA.	2.34
6	BLACK 1 1/4" x 6" NIPPLE	.83	EA.	4.98
1	BLACK 1" x 3/4" REDUCER	.66	EA.	.66
2	BLACK 1 1/4" UNION	3.16	EA.	6.32
2	1 1/4" 24V x 36H GAS RISER	29.80	EA.	59.60
1	BLACK 1 1/2" UNION	4.90	EA.	4.90
ETC.	ETC.	ETC.	ETC.	ETC.
	----------SUBTOTAL----------			$18,000.00

COMMENTS:	SALE AMOUNT	$18,000.00
	MISC. CHARGES	0.00
	FREIGHT	0.00
	SALES TAX	0.00
TERMS: 2%/10th Prox/Net 30th	TOTAL	$18,000.00

5.2 COMMON TYPES OF CASH DISCOUNTS

This is not the only type of cash discount offered to wholesalers. In fact, cash discounts come in many forms. Manufacturers offer a wide range of cash discounts which would include, but not be limited to, 1/2%/10 days net 11, 2%/tenth prox, net 30th, 4%/10 net 11, 2%/90 net 91, and occasionally some seasonal dating where offers would be made in April or May for products delivered in June to be 2% October 30 net October 31, known as extended dating, discussed later in this chapter.

However, the two most common cash discounts are 2%/10 net 30 and 2%/10th prox net 30th. The first, 2%/10 net 30, reads, "two percent, ten days, net thirty days." This means that two percent can be deducted from the invoice as a cash discount if payment is made within ten days from the date of the invoice. This is a standard method in many industries, but has its drawbacks. Because of shipping delays, the wholesaler in many cases will get the invoice but not the material until the 10 days has lapsed. Since most companies will not pay for merchandise until it has been received and checked, the second form of cash discount is more prevalent.

The more common and widely accepted cash discount is 2%/10th prox net 30th which reads "two percent/tenth *prox*, net thirtieth," meaning that two percent may be subtracted from the invoice if payment is made by the tenth of the *month following the present*; however, the full amount of the debt is due and payable on the 30th of the month following the present. The present month would be determined by the date shown on the invoice. If the cash discount is refused, the bill would be due on the 30th of the month following the present.

In accordance, many manufacturers bill their wholesalers on the 25th of the month for the purchases they made, including those from the 26th of the previous month. A wholesaler places an order for galvanized pipe and assorted fittings from the manufacturer on the 26th of May. He orders some additional material on the 15th of June. For these two purchases the wholesaler is invoiced on June 25th. He receives this invoice in the mail on June 29th, marked 2%/10th prox n/30th. This means that 98 percent of the invoice, 100% − 2% discount, must be paid by the tenth day of July in order to earn the cash discount. If the cash discount is refused, the invoice is due and payable in full "net" by the 30th of July.

It is common knowledge that the net profit before tax on an average sale for a wholesaler in a mature industry is usually less than 2%. Because of this low profitability, the cash discount becomes very significant. By taking the cash discount and not passing it on to his customers, the wholesaler has the opportunity to increase his pre-tax profits. For example, if the wholesaler purchased and sold one million dollars in cost of goods sold from inventory in a year, and if all of those goods carried a 2% cash discount which was taken, the wholesaler would save $20,000 in cost of goods for the year. The total cash discounts taken may be a significant part of the profit earned for the entire year.

5.3 WHY CASH DISCOUNTS ARE OFFERED

The question arises, why would a manufacturer want to offer cash discounts of this type to wholesalers? Manufacturers choose to go to market through wholesalers because they can perform the five functions mentioned earlier less expensively than the manufacturers can perform them for themselves. Another pertinent reason they market through distributors is that wholesalers buy the products and usually pay for them in 30 days or so which improves the manufacturer's *cash flow* or reduces the amount of cash the manufacturer needs to run his business.

Imagine if you will the cash that would be needed to support the operation of a manufacturing firm with three hundred sixty five million dollars in sales, provided that the manufacturer takes his product, say carbide cutting tools, to market by the "direct" (not through distributors) method. In addition to the need for extra cash, the manufacturer might have to have a warehouse in every major market area. Not only would he absorb the cost of the warehouse facility, but also the cost of owning the inventory which he had manufactured and stored there.

Cash flow management requires that the manufacturer buy raw materials, manufacture them into finished products, and ship them to their local warehouse to be held until they are sold to the eventual industrial consumer. Let's suppose it takes four months to turn raw material into finished products, and it takes another four months to sell them. To make the cash flow problem worse, it takes another 45 days to collect for the merchandise after it has been sold. This process would consume approximately 9 1/2 months.

On the other hand, should the manufacturer decide to sell his product through local wholesalers, he would not only reduce his cost for owning and operating a local warehouse, but he also reduces his cash requirements significantly because the distributor will buy the inventory and, provided he is given a 2% cash discount, will probably pay for the merchandise within ten to fifteen days. This should shorten the cash flow cycle for the manufacturer by at least 4 to 4 1/2 months. Assuming an eight to nine month cash cycle for the three hundred sixty five million dollar business, the cash requirement has now been reduced by 50 percent by selling through wholesalers. Why? Because the distributor buys the inventory and pays for it within fifteen days. The manufacturer can now reinvest in raw materials, make them into finished goods and sell them again to the wholesaler.

THE FLOW OF CASH

Note! The arrow pointing from the depreciation hour-glass to the cash register needs to be approximately one half the size of the others. This is because the distributor would use cash to purchase capital equipment, depreciate it over time, deduct the amount of the depreciation from income taxes which in essence provides additional cash because it reduced the amount of income tax that would have been paid from cash.

The manufacturing firm with three hundred sixty five million dollars in sales and a four-month turnaround by selling through wholesalers would have a cash requirement average of $1,000,000.00 for each calendar day. Getting the wholesaler to *take the cash discount* 2%/10th prox net 30th, as compared to not taking the discount, would shorten the days receivables for the manufacturer from the 30th of the month to the 10th of the month, or 20 days. This alone would reduce the cash requirement for the manufacturer by $1,000,000.00 X 20 = $20,000,000.00.

This money has a value of almost two million dollars at 10% interest for the year. Therefore, shortening this cash cycle is significant. So much for why cash discounts are offered; let's look at the discount to see whether it should be taken by the wholesaler when it is offered.

5.4 THE IMPORTANCE OF TAKING THE CASH DISCOUNT

Cash discounts are important to profitability. The difference between taking or not taking a cash discount of 2%/10th prox net 30th is the use of the money for an additional 20 days.

Example

Invoice Date	(15 days)	10th Prox	(20 days)	Net Due Date
June 25		July 10th Cash Discount Date		July 30th

In this example, an invoice was received by the wholesaler for $10,000 marked 2%/10th prox and dated June 25th. If the cash discount is to be taken, the bill must be paid by July 10th. If not, it will be due and payable on July 30th. However, by not taking the cash discount and paying the bill "net" on July 30th, the money would be available for use by the wholesaler for an additional 20 days, July 11 - July 30. The question is, what did it cost the wholesaler to use the money the extra 20 days?

A terrible misconception often exists here. When this is discussed with many young branch managers, purchasing managers, and their employees, they assume that 2% per month would garner a total saving of 24% annually. Although this would be a significant saving, it is erroneous because the saving is much greater than that. The following equation may be used to calculate the annual rate of value of the money involved in the cash discount.

Formula for Calculating Discount Values

$$\frac{\text{Discount \%}}{100\% - \text{Discount \%}} \times \frac{365 \text{ days}}{\text{Total Days} - \text{Discount Days}}$$

Examples of the Value of Cash Discounts

1. 2% 10/net 30

The wholesaler receives an invoice dated on the 25th of June. The tenth day is July 5th. In order to take the cash discount, the bill must be paid on that date. In this case we only get to use the supplier's money for 10 days interest free, but we make 37.23% annual rate on our money by taking the cash discount as shown here and provided by applying the formula shown above.

Invoice Date	(10 days)	Discount Date	(20 days)	Net Due Date
June 25		July 5		July 25

$$\frac{2\%}{100\% - 2\%} \times \frac{365}{30 - 10}$$

$$= \frac{.02}{.98^*} \times \frac{365}{20}$$

$$= .0204 \times 18.25$$

= 37.23% annual rate or value of the money.

This is equal to the interest you paid for using the money the extra 20 days if you decided not to take the discount.

*The 98% in the denominator is the money made available from not taking the cash discount.

2. 2% 10th prox / net 30th

In the second case shown here, 2%/10th prox net 30th, the value of the discount would also be 37.23% annual rate, but we would have the added advantage of using the supplier's money interest free for 15 days from June 25th to July 10th even if we decided to take the discount. If we were billed on the 25th of June, the invoice would be payable net the 30th of July.

Invoice Date	(15 days)	Discount Date	(20 days)	Net Due Date
June 25		July 10		July 30

Value of Discount Equals:

$$\frac{\text{Discount \%}}{100\% - \text{Discount \%}} \times \frac{365 \text{ days}}{\text{Total Days} - \text{Discount Days}}$$

$$= \frac{2\%}{100\% - 2\%} \times \frac{365 \text{ Days}}{35 - 15}$$

$$= \frac{.02}{.98} \times \frac{365}{20}$$

$$= .0204 \times 18.25$$

$$= 37.23\%$$

Exercise I

Calculate the cash discount offered and the amount paid as stated in the next problems.

Item	Invoice Amount	Discount Terms	Inv. Date	Date Paid	Amount Paid
1.	$1,790	1/10, n/30	3/1	3/10	$1,772.10
2.	$7,194	2/10, n/30	3/28	4/7	
3.	$5,468	2/10, 1/20, n/30	2/25	3/7	
4.	$2,594	3/10, 1-1/2/15, n/30	7/18	8/17	
5.	$ 135	2-1/2/10, 1-1/2/20, 1/2/30	12/21	1/15	

Exercise II

1. A distributor is invoiced for $58,000 with discounts of 2/10, n/30, on July 28th. The bill is paid on August 8th. How much should be paid?

2. A distributor purchased grinding wheels and was invoiced for $2,303.28 with terms of 2/10, 1-1/2/20, n/30. The invoice was dated May 22nd and payment was made on June 2nd. What is the net amount of the payment?

3. On August 28th, a distributor received an invoice for $34,500 for fiberglass tubing. The terms were 3/10, 1/30, n/60. Payment was made September 7. What is the amount of the discount offered on the day of the payment?

4. A distributor is invoiced on February 20th for $1,195.00 with terms of 2-1/2/10, n/30. Payment is made March 1st.

   What is the amount of the discount?

   What is the amount of the net payment?

5. AAA wholesalers were billed $1,220 for abrasive grain on May 1st with terms of 2/10, 1/30, n/45. The invoice was paid on May 15th. What should be the amount of the payment?

6. The Dependable Plumbing Company purchased equipment invoiced at $7,850.75 from the University Distributing Company on May 27, terms 3/10, n/30. Payment was made June 7.

   What discount should have been taken?

   What was the amount of the payment?

7. On May 26th, Divers Corporation received an invoice amounting to $1,083.75 for materials purchased from Alcoa. The terms of the invoice were 2/10, 1/30, n/60. How much was the amount due on June 6th.

8. The Clark Distributorship purchased electronic components and received an invoice for $7,800 on October 21st with terms of 3/10, 2/30, n/60. They paid the full amount of the bill less the discount on November 1st.

   What was the amount of the discount in dollars?

   What should be the amount paid?

   If payment is made October 31st, what discount can be taken?

5.5 THE ARGUMENT: DO WE DISCOUNT OR PAY LATE?

Some wholesalers would consider not taking the cash discount and paying late instead. They would say that their cost can also be reduced by paying late and thus extending their "interest-free debt" by using the manufacturer's money, interest free, as long as possible. This is not advisable from the standpoint of sound business practices, and these people put their credit rating on the line each time they fail to take a cash discount extended. A cash discount of 2% 10th prox net 30 is equal to a return of 37%, see following chart.

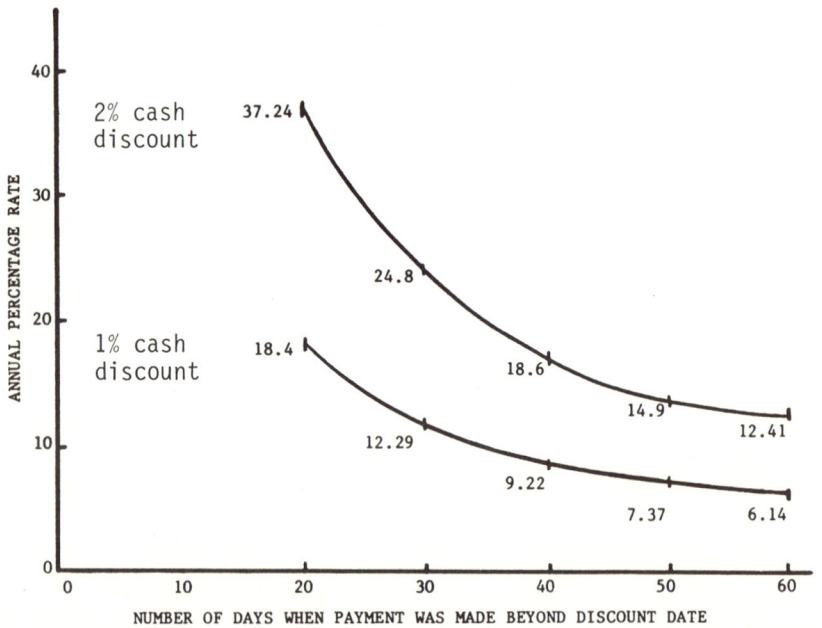

THE HIGH COST OF MISSING THOSE CASH DISCOUNTS

There are few places a wholesaler can make a 37% annual rate on money invested in the business, but taking 2% cash discounts is one of them. The graph's two curves indicate the cost of failing to discount factory invoices. Paying a supplier on the 30th, rather than the 10th, would cost 37% annual rate for the use of the money the extra 20 days.

Bankers would be seriously concerned about the qualifications of any management team that would not take a two percent cash discount. The following explains. Let's suppose a contractor decides not to take the cash discount, but extends payments even beyond the grace period of the 25th or 30th and decides to pay in 45 or even 60 or more days.

The following examples show that by paying in forty-five or even sixty days the cost is significantly higher than the average prime interest rate. This indicates it is good business practice to take a 2% cash discount when these terms are offered.

Value of Discount

45 Days Example

$$= \frac{2\%}{100\% - 2\%} \times \frac{365}{45 - 10}$$

$$= \frac{.02}{.98} \times \frac{365}{35}$$

$$= .0204 \times 10.43$$

$$= 21.3\% \text{ Value of the discount}$$

60 Days Example

$$= \frac{2\%}{100\% - 2\%} \times \frac{365}{60 - 10}$$

$$= \frac{.02}{.98} \times \frac{365}{50}$$

$$= .0204 \times 7.3$$

$$= 14.89\% \text{ Value of the discount}$$

If the value of the money required to take the cash discount is more than the cost of money borrowed at the bank, then the discount should be taken. (See graph of the cost of not taking a cash discount.)

We should note there are not many places in the business where you can make 37% annual rate on your money. However, one way is by taking the 2% cash discounts that are extended to you. In no way can you afford to let these cash discounts pass.

☐ Cost of a missed cash discount on an annual basis, as determined by the value of the money and the number of days beyond the discount date the bill was paid:			Time Between Cash Discount Date And Payment Date		Missing Cash Discount Percentage Cost of	
	Amount of Purchase	Amount of Cash Discount	Number of Days	% of 1 Year	For Any Time Period	On An Annual Basis
2% CASH DISCOUNT:						
Paid 20 Days Beyond	$10,000	$200	20	5.48%	2.0408%	37.24%
Paid 30 Days Beyond	10,000	200	30	8.22	2.0408	24.83
Paid 40 Days Beyond	10,000	200	40	10.96	2.0408	18.62
Paid 50 Days Beyond	10,000	200	50	13.70	2.0408	14.90
Paid 60 Days Beyond	10,000	200	60	16.44	2.0408	12.41
Paid 70 Days Beyond	10,000	200	70	19.18	2.0408	10.64
Paid 80 Days Beyond	10,000	200	80	21.92	2.0408	9.31
Paid 90 Days Beyond	10,000	200	90	24.66	2.0408	8.28
1% CASH DISCOUNT:						
Paid 20 Days Beyond	$10,000	$100	20	5.48	1.0101	18.43
Paid 30 Days Beyond	10,000	100	30	8.22	1.0101	12.29
Paid 40 Days Beyond	10,000	100	40	10.96	1.0101	9.22
Paid 50 Days Beyond	10,000	100	50	13.70	1.0101	7.37
Paid 60 Days Beyond	10,000	100	60	16.44	1.0101	6.14
Paid 70 Days Beyond	10,000	100	70	19.18	1.0101	5.27
Paid 80 Days Beyond	10,000	100	80	21.92	1.0101	4.61
Paid 90 Days Beyond	10,000	100	90	24.66	1.0101	4.10

5.6 DISCOUNTING MAKES MONEY EASIER THAN INCREASING SALES

Cash discounts may be even more important than increased sales. Not only are they more valuable but also easier to obtain. The basic rule is that money can be made more quickly by taking cash discounts than by increasing sales. This is true of the 2% cash discounts offered even if short-term money must be borrowed in order to pay the invoice and take the discounts.

FOR EXAMPLE, A 2% SAVING ON THE COST OF GOODS, WHICH IS WHAT IS ACCOMPLISHED WHEN WE TAKE THE 2% CASH DISCOUNT, IS EQUAL TO A 37.5% INCREASE IN SALES AT 4% NET PROFIT BEFORE TAX, IF WE DO NOT PASS IT THROUGH TO OUR CUSTOMERS.

Assume that a company had annual sales of $1,000,000 and an annual cost of goods of $750,000. The cash discounts, $750,000 × .02, would equal a $15,000 savings if they were taken. In order to make this same $15,000 at 4% net profit before tax we would have to sell an additional $375,000 or a 37.5% increase in sales, $375,000 × .04 = $15,000. Which would be easier: to take the cash discount or to increase your sales by 37.5%?

Another example would be a company which is making a 2% net profit before taxes and has not taken cash discounts in the past. Assuming all of their purchases carried a 2% discount, which they took and did not pass on to their customers, their profits on sales would increase to 3.5%. This is a 75% improvement in pretax profitability for this company.

Proof: Sales = $1,000,000   COGS = $750,000

Profits = $1,000,000 × .02 = $20,000

New COGS = $750,000 × .98 = $735,000, a $15,000 improvement

New profits = $20,000 + $15,000 = $35,000 = 3.5% profit on sales

Profit Improvement = $(3.5 - 2) \div 2 = 75\%$

Three other reasons exist for taking cash discounts. First, it is not uncommon for wholesalers who discount their bills to have a better credit rating and receive even more prompt service and response from their suppliers. The second reason is to indicate your financial knowledge to your supplier as well as to your banker. Most bankers are critical of managers who do not take the cash discounts offered.

In addition, firms who regularly discount their bills (take cash discounts) may be in position to negotiate for extended terms from their manufacturers. An example would be paying in 30 to 60 days but still taking the cash discount.

5.7 PASSING THROUGH THE DISCOUNT

Many wholesalers who receive cash discounts of 2% pass that same 2% discount on to their customers. In discussions with them, they make statements like, "Well, we get a two percent discount, so we provided that same 2% cash discount to our customers." This is not wrong, but it sure is expensive.

Suppose materials were purchased for $10,000 for a certain construction project, and the wholesaler took a 2% cash discount which was equal to $200. The distributor sells the material for $12,500 with a gross margin of 20% and offers a cash discount of 2%. Two percent of $10,000 is $200; however, 2% of $12,500 is $250. A smooth exchange, but fifty dollars was lost in the transaction. Why? Two percent of a smaller number, the purchased price, is less than 2% of a larger number, the selling price. You may choose to pass through the cash discounts, but in your planning for profit, at least you need to realize you are losing money when you pass on the same discount you received from your suppliers.

5.8 CASH DISCOUNTS AND EXTENDED DATING

Cash discounts are profitable and should be taken. However, with the manufacturer's permission, the distributor can enjoy using "extended dating," and the use of the manufacturer's interest free money, and still earn a cash discount.

Extended dating is acceptable to the manufacturer when it is in their benefit. You should ask for extended dating if: you have an exceptionally good credit rating, your volume and credit combination justify it, you are buying seasonal items to be sold at a later date, if the manufacturer wants you to open a branch in another city to help them gain or hold market share, if your ability to forecast product usage reduces the manufacturers costs of doing business with you.

Other reasons for allowing extended dating would include, when sales are slow, such as in times of recession, when the manufacturer has inventory on hand he wants to move now, and to secure future orders in order to keep plants in production. Such terms will generally only be offered to wholesalers who have excellent credit and who always discount their invoices (take cash discounts).

Extended terms would mean that the distributor would have several extra days to pay their bills and still earn a cash discount. An example of extended dating would be 2%/90 net 120. This extends the payment period for taking the cash discount from 15 to 90 days. Although the value of the discount decreases from 31% to 25% in this example, we have the added advantage of the 90 day interest-free debt.

2%/90 net 120 Equals:

$$= \frac{2\%}{100\% - 2\%} \times \frac{365}{120 - 90}$$

$$= \frac{.02}{.98} \times \frac{365}{30}$$

$$= .0204 \times 12.17$$

$$= 25\%$$

An example of seasonal dating would be, if material was purchased in May and billed May 25th (2% 90 net 120), the invoice would be due and payable on the 23rd of August in order to take the cash discount.

If the wholesaler is doing $10,000 per month in business with this manufacturer, the extended dating is like getting a $30,000 interest-free loan from the manufacturer without forfeiting the cash discount. This $30,000 at 10% interest for one year has a value of $3,000 or $300 per month. It's worth asking for.

To determine the actual value of the interest-free debt, have your branch managers reduce the dollar amount invested in inventory in their branches by the amount of the payables they owe. This is justifiable because of the interest-free nature of the debt. Then, when these numbers are plugged into the return on assets managed formula, shown in chapter 8, (Dupont ROI Model), it will be quite evident that the return on assets managed will be significantly improved.

Example

Constant Construction Supply Company purchases $6,800 worth of material and is invoiced for this amount and offered terms of 2%/10th prox net 30th. The bill must be paid by the tenth of the month following the month in which the invoice was dated if the cash discount is to be taken. The amount of the cash discount is calculated by using the formula "the invoice amount x the discount rate is equal to the discount in dollars." Thus the amount due is equal to the invoice price minus the discount.

We must first decide to take the cash discount and then do the following calculation: $6,800 X .02 = $136. This payment, of course, would not be made prior to the 10th of the following month so that the wholesaler could use the money as long as possible, interest free. Remember, this is the only interest-free debt the distributor enjoys. The amount to be paid would be $6,800 X .98 = $6,664.

Some manufacturers offer mixed discounts to their wholesalers. For example, a distributor purchased electrical switch gear and was invoiced for $9,700 on March 29th. The terms of payment were 3/10, 2/20, n/30. Payment was made April 9th. What was the amount of the discount allowed?

A good rule to remember when calculating cash discounts is "30 days hath September, April, June and November; all the others have 31 except February which has 28 and sometimes 29" (author unknown). Since March has 31 days, payment on April 9th includes two days in March and nine days in April, a total of eleven days which justifies only the 2% discount. Had the bill been paid on April 8th, the 3% discount could have been taken and should have been. It is not uncommon in some industries for a wholesaler to get invoiced for 3%/30, 2%/60, net 90. The first discount should generally be taken even if money must be borrowed.

Exercise I

1. On the purchase of abrasive wheels, discounts of 20% and 5% are received; terms of purchase are 2/10, n/30. The distributor is invoiced $2,300 for 100 abrasive wheels. Payment for the wheels is made within 10 days. What is the distributor's cost per abrasive wheel?

2. The Ace Distribution Corporation buys 10 electronic monitors at a list price of $150 each on May 4th. They are offered discounts of 18% and 22% from the manufacturer with terms of 3/10, n/30.

   What amount should the distributor pay on May 14th?

   What single multiplier could be used to calculate the invoice price?

   If the interest rate is 11% (annual rate) and the loan can be repaid in 45 days, how much money will the distributor save on the purchase by borrowing the money and taking the discount?

3. The ABC Company received a shipment of oil field equipment for which the list price was $95,785. This was subject to discounts of 15%, 10%, 5%, and 2.5% and terms of 2/10, 1-1/2/20, and n/30. The invoice was dated March 24th and payment was made on April 3rd. What was the total amount paid?

4. A distributor purchased a pallet of threaded fasteners which listed for $52,021 and carried trade discounts of 11%, 7%, and 1%. They were invoiced on January 26th and offered cash discounts of 2-1/2/10, 1/30.

   How much was the invoice?

   How much should they pay on 2/26?

   Should they borrow the money and take the maximum cash discount if the interest rate is 1-1/2% per month and the loan can be repaid in 75 days?

5. Triplett Construction calls a local distributor and requests a bid on 19 units of scaffolding. The buyer is informed that the list price is $118.50 per unit, and his trade discount will be 5% and 2-1/2%. An additional 2-1/2% will be extended if the order is for 5 packages of 4 units and 2% if paid in 10 days. He purchased the 5 standard packages.

   What was the amount of the invoice?

   What single multiplying factor can be used to determine the amount of the expected invoice?

   What was the dollar amount of the trade discount?

   What percent of the list price is the trade discount?

   How much money would the contractor save by borrowing money at an annual rate of 12% in order to take the cash discount, providing repayment could be made in 75 days?

Chapter 6

Markups

In the chapter on cash discounts we said that many products are purchased and sold from manufacturer suggested resale (list) price sheets. The wholesaler buys and resells from these sheets, taking and giving various discounts from the list price. For the sake of quick review, let's suppose that a distributor purchases a whirlpool bath that carries a suggested list price of $2,400, with trade discounts of 25%, 20%, and 10%. The wholesaler then sells the whirlpool to a contractor customer at $2,400 less discounts of 20% and 10%.

The distributor would therefore pay $2,400 × .75 × .80 × .90 = $1,296.00.

The customer would pay: $2,400 × .80 × .90 = $1,728.00.

The difference between the selling price of $1,728.00 and the cost of $1,296.00 would be the wholesaler's gross margin in dollars:

$1,728 − $1,296 = $432.00, or 25% of the selling price.

These calculations are simple enough when the list price is provided by the manufacturer, and the gross margin required by the distributor is known. However, life is never consistently this straightforward. Additional problems arise, for example, with a special order accompanied by only the vendor's invoice stating what we, the wholesaler, paid for the material.

Let's suppose we know that the particular customer for this special order is accustomed to receiving trade discounts to meet the local market conditions. In addition, he may expect a "large user" or some other common discount. We should also know the required gross margin for the sale to be profitable. The question is: How do we mark up an item so that the invoice to the contractor provides the discounts he expects, while still leaving us the required gross margin? First, we need to understand the difference between the formulas for percent markup and percent gross margin.

Percent Markup From invoice Cost

$$= \frac{\text{Selling Price} - \text{COGS}}{\text{COGS}} \times 100$$

Percent Gross Margin

$$= \frac{\text{Selling Price} - \text{COGS}}{\text{Selling Price}} \times 100$$

Let's calculate the percent markup and the percent gross margin for a situation in which the selling price is $100, the gross margin is $20, the cost of goods sold (COGS) is $80, and the markup is $20

Percent Markup $= \dfrac{\$100 - \$80}{\$80} \times 100 = 25\%$

Markup in dollars $= \$100 - \$80 = \$20$

Percent Gross Margin $= \dfrac{\$100 - \$80}{\$100} \times 100 = 20\%$

Gross Margin $= \$100 - \$80 = \$20$

Notice that even though both the gross margin and the markup are $20, the percent gross margin is 20% while the percent markup is 25%. Yes, it is true that a 20% gross margin is equal to a 25% markup. They are equal because we are calculating the percentage of two different numbers; the cost of goods sold for the markup and the selling price for the gross margin.

The next question is, if the markup and the gross margin are the same in dollars, but have different percentages, how can we determine the markup when we have already determined the gross margin?

6.1 HOW TO CALCULATE PERCENT GROSS MARGIN WHEN PERCENT MARKUP IS KNOWN

A distributor has instructed the pricing clerk to mark up each item 25% of the invoice price. An item is purchased and invoiced at $80. Thus:

$80 X .25 = $20 Markup
$80 + $20 = $100 Selling price

The gross margin in dollars is equal to the markup in dollars, as shown below:

Selling Price — COGS = Gross Margin

$100.00 − $80.00 = $20.00 Gross Margin
$80.00 + (80 X .25) = $20.00 Markup

But what percent of the selling price above is gross margin?

$$\text{Percent Gross Margin} = \frac{\text{Percent Markup}}{100\% + \text{Percent Markup}} \times 100$$

$$= \frac{25\% \text{ Markup}}{100\% + 25\% \text{ Markup}} \times 100$$

$$= \frac{.25}{1 + .25} \times 100$$

$$= 20\%$$

Therefore, a 25% markup is equal to a 20% gross margin because a larger percent of a smaller number (the cost) is equal to a smaller percent of a larger number (the selling price).

Keep in mind that the gross margin is not profit. Gross margin dollars are used to pay employees, finance inventory and receivables, and otherwise pay for all selling and operating expenses. The remaining profit before all taxes are paid (called "net profit before taxes") may be as small as 2% or 3% of sales even when the overall gross margin is 25%.

It is also true and can be calculated by the formulas shown

above that a 100% markup and a 50% discount represent the same dollar volume. It is quite common in retail sales of clothing, jewelry and furniture to find goods marked up 100% to 200% or more. For example a lady's suit is purchased by the clothier for $200.00 and is marked to sell at $400.00, a 100% markup. After some time the suit has not sold and is put "on sale" with a discount of 50%, $400 X .50 = $200, or the retailer's cost of the goods.

Because the retailer's original markup was 100%, some would say: "The clothier is making a 100% profit!"- a common mistake of those misinformed about the retail and wholesale industries. A 100% profit is impossible. Even if the goods were acquired free, the cost of handling and selling would use at least part of the 100%.

Incidentally, most wholesalers in mature industries make about 20% to 25% gross margin on stock sales and many unfortunately accept a net profit after taxes of 1.5% to 2% when calculated as a percentage of sales.

Exercise 1

Using the formula for calculating the percent gross margin when the percent markup is known, calculate the percent gross margin on the following.

Percent Markup	Percent Gross Margin
11.11	10
17.65	
25.00	
33.33	
42.86	
53.86	
66.67	
80.00	
100.00	

6.2 HOW TO CALCULATE PERCENT MARKUP WHEN PERCENT GROSS MARGIN IS KNOWN

Consider this example: A distributor's purchasing manager buys an item to be drop shipped to the customer and is invoiced for $75. Her company's policy is to make 25% gross margin on every drop shipment item. How much does she tell the pricing clerk to mark up the $75.00 invoiced price of the item? NOTE: Remember that gross margin is always calculated on the selling price.

$$\text{Percent Markup} = \frac{\text{Percent Gross Margin}}{100\% - \text{PGM}} \times 100$$

$$= \frac{25\%}{100\% - 25\%} \times 100$$

$$= \frac{.25}{.75} \times 100$$

$$= 33.33\%$$

Selling Price = COGS + Markup

$$= \$75 + (\$75 \times .3333)$$
$$= \$75 + \$25 = \$100.00$$

Exercise I

Using the formula for finding the percent markup when the desired percent gross margin is known, calculate the percent markups in the following problems.

Desired Percent Gross Margin	Percent Markup
9	10
11	
12	
16	
18	
26	
32	
46	

Exercise II

Using the formulas shown above, calculate the percent markup, the markup in dollars and the selling price of the following items:

COGS	Percent Gross Margin	Percent Markup	Markup in Dollars	Selling Price
$ 100	20	25	25	$125
$ 119	18			
$ 644	9			
$5,282	13-1/2			
$ 755	27			
$9,576	31			
$ 813	38			
$ 227	5-1/4			
$3,691	49			

Exercise III

1. A distributor placed a large order for standard lighting fixtures with a local manufacturer. The fixtures are to be "drop shipped" (shipped by the manufacturer directly to the customer's location). The entire order of fixtures costs the distributor $118,000. He wants to make a 5% gross margin on the sale.

   Find the percent markup.

   Find the selling price of the fixtures.

2. A distributor received a rush order from a customer for an item which was not in inventory. In order to serve the customer, the distributor decided to "buy the item out" (purchase from a local competitor). The cost of the item to the distributor was $142.00. The distributor wanted to make a 9% gross margin on buy-out items.

   Find the percent markup.

Find the dollar value of the markup.

3. A distributor ordered a special machinery repair part for a customer. The part was received along with an invoice for $701.00. The distributor wants to make a 28% gross margin on the sale of special orders.

   Calculate the percent markup.

   Find the markup in dollars.

   Determine the selling price.

4. A distributor purchased 50 containers of rig wash. Thirty of these were presold at 21% gross margin. The cost to the distributor was $57.00 each.

   Calculate the percent markup.

   Determine the selling price of the 30 cases.

5. A distributor purchased an electric motor for $81.00, an air compressor for $730.00 and an air storage tank for $316.00. The desired gross margin is 25% on the motor, 18% on the compressor and 20% on the tank.

   Calculate the percent markup for each item.

   Calculate the combined selling price if the three units are sold as a package on one invoice.

6.3 HOW TO CALCULATE PERCENT MARKUP WHEN THE COGS AND SELLING PRICE ARE KNOWN

It is often necessary to calculate the percent markup when the selling price and cost of goods sold are known. For example, in a distributorship where prices are generally calculated from cost, a middle manager might be questioned by a customer about an invoice price. The manager has the selling price and quickly looks up the cost of goods sold. In order to ascertain whether the selling price is correct, the percent markup is calculated to see that it coincides with the markup normally given this customer. The formula below is applied:

Percent Markup

$$= \frac{\text{Selling Price} - \text{COGS}}{\text{COGS}} \times 100$$

$$= \frac{\$125 - 100}{\$100} \times 100$$

$$= 25\%$$

Again, keep in mind that the markup in dollars is equal to the gross margin in dollars, but the percentages are different.

Exercise I

Using the formula for calculating the percent markup when the COGS and Selling Price are known, calculate the percent markup in each of the following:

Selling Price	COGS	Percent Markup
$ 150.00	$ 100.00	50%
$ 10.00	$ 8.10	
$1,140.25	$1,000.00	
$ 980.17	$ 615.90	
$ 712.00	$ 436.49	
$3,960.69	$2,999.99	
$ 4.25	$ 2.01	
$ 11.79	$ 3.50	
$2,466.38	$2,155.25	
$ 800.00	$ 715.00	

6.4 HOW TO CALCULATE SELLING PRICE FROM COGS USING THE DIVISOR PRINCIPLE

There is a simplified method of calculating the selling price directly from the cost of goods sold. This eliminates the need for calculating the markup in dollars and then adding this amount to the cost of goods sold (shown earlier). This divisor formula can be used when the cost of goods sold and the percent gross margin desired are known. For example, a distributor purchases electronic components for $230 and wants to make a 24% gross margin on the sale. To find the selling price he can use the following method:

Selling Price

$$= \frac{COGS}{100\% - \text{Percent Gross Margin}}$$

$$= \frac{\$230}{100\% - 24\%}$$

$$= \frac{\$230}{.76}$$

$$= \$302.63$$

Basically, this is the same percentage formula you learned earlier. The cost of goods sold at $230 (the "percentage") is 76% (the "rate") of some unknown ("base") number.

$$\text{Base} = \frac{\text{Percentage}}{\text{Rate}}$$

$$= \frac{\$230}{100\% - 24\%}$$

$$= \frac{\$230}{76\% \text{ or } .76}$$

$$= \$302.63 = \text{Selling Price}$$

For the most common gross margins, the calculation of the rate can be done mentally. For example, calculating the divisor factor used to find an item's selling price with a desired gross margin percent of 21.5% is simply a matter of subtraction:

100% − 21.5% =

1 − .215 = .785

Exercise I

Calculate and insert below the proper "divisors" required to ascertain the selling price when the COGS and the desired percent gross margin are known.

Desired Percent Gross Margin	Divisor	COGS	Selling Price
5	.95	$ 149	$156.84
7-1/2		$ 388	
11		$ 955	
14		$ 251	
20		$7,591	
31-1/3		$4,472	
37		$1,873	
40		$ 776	
41-3/8		$ 339	
25		$ 314	

However, to eliminate errors, a table of divisors (see chart) can be calculated and divisors simply "pulled off the sheet" and used in the formula.

Exercise II

Make a chart and insert the divisors which an employee could use to find the selling price of any item with gross margin between 18 and 25 percent. Use only whole percentage points.

HOW TO PRICE FOR PROFIT

To make a gross margin of	DIVISOR Divide the cost of goods sold by	or	MULTIPLIER Multiply the cost of goods by
5%	.95		1.0526
6%	.94		1.0638
7%	.93		1.0753
8%	.92		1.0869
9%	.91		1.0989
10%	.90		1.1111
11%	.89		1.1236
12%	.88		1.1364
13%	.87		1.1494
14%	.86		1.1628
15%	.85		1.7647
16%	.84		1.1905
17%	.83		1.2048
18%	.82		1.2195
19%	.81		1.2346
20%	.80		1.2500
21%	.79		1.2658
22%	.78		1.2821
23%	.77		1.2987
24%	.76		1.3158
25%	.75		1.3333
26%	.74		1.3514
27%	.73		1.3699
28%	.72		1.3889
29%	.71		1.4085
30%	.70		1.4286
31%	.69		1.4493
32%	.68		1.4706
33%	.67		1.4925
34%	.66		1.5151
35%	.65		1.5385
36%	.64		1.5625
37%	.63		1.5873
38%	.62		1.6129
39%	.61		1.6393
40%	.60		1.6666
41%	.59		1.6949
42%	.58		1.7241
43%	.57		1.7544
44%	.56		1.7857
45%	.55		1.8182
46%	.54		1.8519
47%	.53		1.8868
48%	.52		1.9231
49%	.51		1.9608
50%	.50		2.0000

6.5 HOW TO CALCULATE SELLING PRICE FROM COGS USING THE MULTIPLIER PRINCIPLE

The numbers in the third column of the chart were calculated using the following formula:

$$\text{Multiplier} = 1 + \frac{\text{Gross Margin}}{1 - \text{Gross Margin}}$$

In other words, to make a gross margin of 5% on the price, the cost must be multiplied by 1.0526.

$$\begin{aligned}
\text{Multiplier} &= 1 + \frac{5\%}{1.00 - .05} \\
&= 1 + \frac{.05}{1.00 - .05} \\
&= \frac{.05}{.95} \\
&= 1.0526
\end{aligned}$$

If the multiplier you desire is not on the sheet, it can be quickly calculated by the formula. For example, for a 21.5% gross margin:

$$\begin{aligned}
\text{Multiplier} &= 1 + \frac{21.5\%}{1.00 - 21.5\%} \\
&= 1 + \frac{.215}{.785} \\
&= 1.2739
\end{aligned}$$

Thus, the selling price of an item costing the wholesaler $16 assuming a gross margin of 21.5%, would be

$$\begin{aligned}
\text{Selling Price} &= \text{COGS} \times \text{Multiplier} \\
&= \$16 \times 1.2739 \\
&= \$20.38
\end{aligned}$$

Multiple markups using the multiplier are more likely to be erroneous, due to their complexity, than are calculations using divisors. The selling price of a $16 item can be more easily calculated by dividing the cost of goods sold by the divisor factor .785 (which again, can be mentally calculated: $1 - .215$).

$$\text{Selling Price} = \frac{\text{COGS}}{\text{Divisor Factor}}$$

$$= \frac{\$16}{.785}$$

$$= \$20.38$$

6.6 HOW TO CALCULATE MULTIPLE MARKUPS FROM COST

Because many buyers are accustomed to list-less-discounts purchasing, some distributors calculate these even when dealing with an invoice showing their cost. The divisor principle is also useful in dealing with multiple markups which are necessary to ascertain the list price from a known cost of goods sold. This is especially true when the distributor extends discounts to the customer from the list price.

For example, a distributor purchases a special product for a customer for $117.00. Because it is a small sale of a specialty item, the distributor wants to make a gross margin of 35% on the selling price after allowing a 10% trade discount to the customer. The inside salesperson must be able to calculate 1) the list price, 2) the selling price to the customer after allowing the discount, and 3) the gross margin in dollars.

In order to determine the list price, we must perform a two-step operation:

Step 1: The selling price is 100% – 35%, or 65% of some unknown number. In other words, .65 is our divisor in this problem.

$$\text{Selling Price} = \frac{\text{COGS}}{100\% - 35\%}$$
$$= \frac{\$117}{.65}$$
$$= \$180$$

Step 2: Use the selling price to find the list price. The selling price of $180 is 100% minus the 10% trade discount or 90% of some unknown number:

$$\text{List Price} = \frac{\text{Selling Price}}{100\% - 10\%}$$
$$= \frac{\$180}{.90}$$
$$= \$200$$

List Price − Trade Discount = Selling Price

Selling Price = $200 − ($200 × 10%)
             = $200 − $20
             = $180

List Price - Discount - Gross Margin = COGS

             = $200 − ($200 × .10) - ($180 × .35)
             = $200 − $20 − $63
             = $117

The divisors used to find the list price may be multiplied together to get one divisor without changing their cumulative value: .65 × .90 = .585. The total formula would be $117 ÷ .65 ÷ .90, or $117 ÷ .585 = $200.

Let's suppose that this same customer also always requests and takes a 2% cash discount. However, because of the extra effort expended in ordering and handling the small-dollar-volume item, the distributor must make a 35% margin after all trade and cash discounts were taken.

The formula would then be:

$117 ÷ .65 ÷ .90 ÷ .98 = $204.08 List Price

The .98 divisor in the formula represents the markup to allow the 2% cash discount and still earn the 35% margin required.

When working from cost and using the markup system, to find the selling price we must always calculate the markup to allow for returns or discounts taken and other factors affecting profitability. If, for example, our operating costs are 21% of sales and we are trying to make 2% net profit before tax, we would calculate the gross margin at 23%. However, if a customer takes our normal 2% cash discount, we would work hard to provide a good service, but make no net profit on this sale because we gave it away in the cash discount. Care should be taken when marking up from a known cost of goods that the total cost of doing business, plus a reasonable profit, are covered by the selling price.

Exercise I

Using the previously discussed method, calculate the unknown in the problems shown below.

1. A distributor is invoiced $25 for a raised face weld-neck flange. The gross margin is to be 18%. Calculate the selling price.

2. A lathe tool holder costs a distributor $83. The distributor plans to make a 40% gross margin. What would be the selling price?

3. A distributor bought a saw for $175 and wanted to make a gross margin of 31-1/2%. Find the selling price.

4. A distributor bought a set of tools for $170 and wants to make a gross margin of 26-1/4%. Find the selling price.

5. A distributor purchases a used N/C mill for $75,750 and wants to make a gross margin of 23% on the sale.

    Find the selling price.

    Find the gross margin in dollars.

6. A special electronic instrument is purchased by a distributor for $856.50. When the item sells, the company wants to make a gross margin of 17-1/3%.

    Find the selling price.

    Find the gross margin in dollars.

7. A distributor's cost of goods is $17,693 and the gross margin is to be 6-2/3%.

    Find the selling price.

    Find the gross margin in dollars.

8. The purchasing manager for a construction firm bought a crane for 37.5% off list price. The crane cost the firm $87,500.

What was the list price?

How much was the discount in dollars?

9. A commercial rental firm paid 18% down on a truck. The down payment was $1,623. The company received a 20% trade discount.

   Find the list price.

   Find the selling price.

10. A Civil Construction Company bought three fork lifts on sale for 15% and 5% off list. The fork lift trucks cost $24,000 each.

    Find the list price for the three trucks.

    Find the dollar saving by acquiring the additional 5% discount.

11. A manufacturer's list price on scaffolding shows sales subject to a lead discount of 20% and subsequent discounts of 5% and 4-1/2%, depending upon volume purchased.

    Find the list price of 100 units which cost $78.50 each with discounts of 20% and 5%.

    Find the list price of 120 units which cost $75 each but received all 3 discounts. If they could be sold to a customer with a trade discount of 15%, What would be the dollar difference between the two transactions per unit?

12. A distributor is invoiced for $9,572 for a high-pressure pump. The pump is for a customer who receives trade discounts of 15% and 5% and a cash discount of 2% which is always taken. The distributor wants to make a gross margin of 17% on the net price.

    Find the list price provided the customer.

    Find the net price paid by the customer.

    Find the dollar amount of the trade and cash discounts combined.

6.7 TRADE PRICING

The formulas presented in this chapter are particularly useful in a pricing technique now being adopted by certain manufacturers. Called "trade pricing" or "matrix pricing," it is a substitute for the "list price, less discounts" pricing method. The latter encourages buyers to seek a list price and then shop around for the best discount from list. Trade pricing, on the other hand, is a markup from a confidential distributor cost.

The purpose of trade pricing is to give the distributor a substantially higher gross margin on slower moving inventory items. The distribution goal is to make a gross margin return on inventory investment (GMROII) of $1.50 to $2.00 for every one dollar invested in inventory.

$$\text{GMROII} = \frac{\text{Inventory Turn} \times \text{Percent Gross Margin}}{1 - \text{Percent Gross Margin}}$$

Using this formula the distributor would earn $1.71 of gross margin on an item which turned only 4 times and earned a 30 percent gross margin.

$$\text{GMROII} = \frac{4 \times .30}{1 - .30}$$

$$= \frac{1.20}{.70}$$

$$= \$1.71$$

Approximately the same gross margin, $1.75, would be earned on sales with a lower margin if the item could be turned faster. For example, on commodity products it is common for the supply to be relatively high and the demand to be somewhat lower than the supply. This is a common cause of lower prices. When an item cannot be sold for more than 20 percent gross margin then to earn $1.75 in gross margin for every dollar invested in inventory the product must be turned seven times.

$$\text{GMROII} = \frac{7 \times .20}{.80}$$

$$= \$1.75$$

Although problems may arise for a wholesaler when dealing with contractor-buyers steeped in list-price purchasing, these problems may be overcome to the distributor's advantage.

Trade pricing benefits to the distributor include:

1. The opportunity for the customer to compare value, not suppliers' various discounts from a standard list price.

2. The ability to set higher gross margins on slower moving items.

3. The opportunity to price from a known distributor cost according to product movement.

4. The occasion to vary margins in a standard three-column price sheet, each column reflecting customer buying habits.

5. The chance to price for higher gross margins on small sales and broken-carton amounts.

6. The ability to increase overall profitability for a particular line.

Potential disadvantages include:

1. The distributor salesmen may shave selling prices too close as a result of their knowing company costs.

2. Confidential cost information could end up in buyers' hands.

3. Possible conflicts could arise with buyers who have traditionally purchased by "list price, less discounts".

Chapter 7

Interest

The saying "Cash is King" means that available cash is the life blood of any company. Well managed distributorships are continually planning the flow of their cash so they have money readily available to pay operating expenses, salaries and benefits for their employees, suppliers for purchased inventory and to pay interest on borrowed funds. Most wholesaler-distributors know that sooner or later even the best financed company will need to borrow money to pay current expenses or to finance long term growth.

Short term loans are usually associated with daily operating funds and are financed with funds coming into the company from receivables or by borrowing from a bank or other lender against these receivables or inventory. Long term debt is usually used to finance the purchase of capital equipment or to finance a higher level of growth than can be funded from current retained earnings (monies after taxes which can be reinvested back into the business).

When a company or individual borrows money, interest is charged by the lending institution for the use of their depositors money. In the material that follows we will examine how interest is calculated. We will restrict our discussion to the simpler types of loans which would likely be used by a company which has the financial potential to pay its bills but needs ready cash, and to the taking of personal loans by individuals.

7.1 SIMPLE INTEREST FORMULA

When a distributor borrows short term money from a bank it would ordinarily pay simple interest at a rate of one or two percentage points over the prime lending rate (the rate the larger banks charge their best customers). For example, if the Bank of America is charging Motorola 8 percent, then the distributor would usually pay a rate of nine, ten or eleven percent, depending upon how much risk the bank decided they were taking in making the loan. The interest rate would usually be simple interest which will be discussed here.

Simple interest is calculated by the formula:

$I = P \times R \times T$

I represents the interest to be paid.
P is the amount of the loan (principal).
R is the rate or the percent interest charged.
T is the time element involved in years or fraction of a year.

Example

Calculate the interest charged a distributor who borrowed $10,000 for 30 days at 11%.

Formula

$I = P \times R \times T$
$I = \$10,000 \times 11\% \times 30/365$
$I = \$10,000 \times .11 \times .0822$
$I = \$90.41$

Exercise I

Find the amount of interest a distributor must pay on each of the following loans and calculate the total amount owed on the date of payment.

Amount	Percent	Number of Days	Interest	Amount Due
$ 750.00	5	365	$37.50	$787.50
$ 900.00	6	90		
$ 1,215.00	7-1/2	45		
$18,518.00	10-1/4	180		
$ 6,637.00	8-3/8	210		
$ 5,000.00	14	480		
$ 6,000.00	6	60		
$ 381.00	18	30		
$ 8,163.00	12-1/8	310		
$ 900.00	16-1/2	115		

7.2 SINGLE PAYMENT NOTES

It is the opinion of the author that as a general rule well established companies should not have to borrow money. They should make sufficient profits and retain earnings to reinvest in the company to sustain a ten percent growth rate with no borrowed funds. If they must borrow money from time to time then simple interest notes (loans) are the appropriate type to attain.

The reason is that on simple interest, single payment notes, with no required payment structure other than a single payment at the end of the note period, any amount paid on the principal before the note is due stops the interest paid on the amount paid as of the date of the payment.

Example

A distributor who is short of cash borrows $5,000 to take advantage of a 2% cash discount offered on merchandise purchased. The note is a single payment note payable in 60 days at 11% annual rate.

However, the distributor receives accounts receivable sooner than expected and applies $2,000 to the note 15 days after the note was made, and another $2,000 30 days from the date of the original note. The other $1,000 is paid at the maturity date of 60 days.

Find the amount of interest paid:

Formula:

$I = P \times R \times T$

Step 1

Calculate interest to date of the first payment.

$I = \$5,000 \times 11\% \times 15/365$
$ = \$5,000 \times .11 \times .0411$
$ = \$22.60$

Step 2

Reduce the note by the amount paid and calculate the interest due at the second payment period.

$5,000 - $2,000 = $3,000 Balance

I = $3,000 X 11% X 15/365
  = $3,000 X .11 X .0411
  = $13.56

Step 3

Reduce the note by the additional $2,000 paid. The remaining $1,000 on the note was paid in the full 60 days from the date of the original note, or 30 days after the last payment.

I = $1,000 X 11% X 30/365
  = $1,000 X .11 X .0822
  = $9.04

Total interest paid was:

Total interest = $22.60 + $13.56 + $9.04
  = $45.20

How much money did the distributor save by making premature payments on the note?
Interest for the full 60 days would have been:

I = P X R X T
  = $5,000 X 11% X 60 days
  = $5,000 X .11 X 60/365
  = $5,000 X .11 X .1644
  = $90.42

The saving was:

$$90.42 - 45.20 = 45.22$$

or $\frac{45.22}{90.42} = 50\%$

In calculating the interest paid on the notes in the following exercise, assume that the days held represent the actual days for which the borrower paid interest on that particular amount. If the note was held 15 days, payment was made, then held an additional 60 days, then the maturity date was 75 days from the date of the original note.

Exercise I

Calculate the total interest paid on the following notes:

Original Loan	Annual Rate%	1st Payment Amount	Days	2nd Payment Amount	Days	Total Interest
$ 5,000.00	10	$ 2,000	15	$ 3,000	60	$69.87
$ 819.00	9	$ 819	75			
$ 1,274.00	12	$ 637	180	$ 637	360	
$28,010.00	9-1/2	$ 8,010	60	$20,000	90	
$ 7,500.00	11-1/8	$ 2,500	36	$ 5,000	58	
$89,890.00	8-3/4	$46,000	40	$43,890	80	
$ 3,115.00	14	$ 1,000	10	$ 2,115	180	
$ 1,790.00	13-1/3	$ 1,790	90			
$14,212.00	18	$10,000	27	$ 4,212	42	
$ 3,600.00	8-1/4	$ 600	15	$ 3,000	45	

7.3 ADD-ON INTEREST

Many loan companies and some banking institutions, in order to collect the interest portion of loans sooner, have for years used an interest charge system called "add-on" interest. This system is more prevalent in the consumer lending market than in commercial loans generally received by distributors. It is to every borrower's advantage to be aware of this system when purchasing consumer goods on credit. In the example show here we are using the add-on interest rate. One thousand dollars was borrowed from a loan company for 12 months. The add-on interest rate is 7%.

Rule of thumb:

(Add-on Interest Rate X 2) − 1 = Approximate Simple Interest Rate

Example

(7% add-on X 2) − 1 = 13% Simple Interest*

*The exact rate is 12.68%, but the rule of thumb will give you a close approximation. The effective interest rate is higher because the borrower on a monthly payment plan does not have use of the entire amount of money for the full period of the loan. Most states have truth-in-lending laws which require that the lending institution disclose to the borrower the affective simple interest rate in their advertisements when add-on interest is being charged.

How the system works: On the one-year note described above, a system called "The Rule of 78's" is applied. Twelve equal payments will be established, each containing payments applied first to the interest, then to the principal. At the time of the first payment, the borrower would pay 12÷78, or 15% of the total interest due for the year. At the end of the fourth month, in one-third of the repayment period, 54% of the interest would have been paid, as shown in the following chart. The same basic formula applies to loans of longer duration. Two-year (24 month) notes use the rule of 300 while the rule of 666 applies to 36-month loans. The same reasoning applies in calculating the interest paid each month.

Example

$\dfrac{36}{666}$ = 5.41% of total interest paid the first month

$\dfrac{1}{666}$ = 0.15% of the interest paid the last month

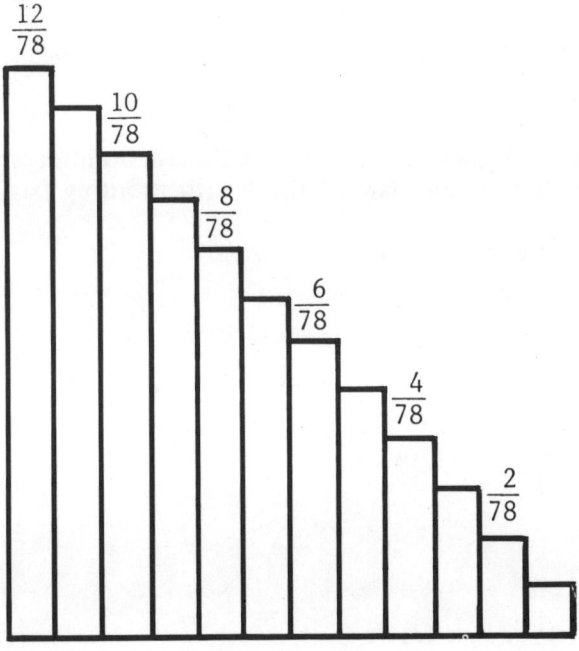

The rules of 78, 300 and 666 are formulated by adding the total number of months for which the loan is made.

Example

Rule of 78 = Sum of the number of months in the repayment agreement.

$$1 + 2 + 3 + 4 + 5 + 6 + 7 + 8 + 9 + 10 + 11 + 12 = 78$$

If you plan to pay your note in the time frame specified, you do not wish to pay the note off sooner and save some of the interest you would other wise pay then it makes no real difference to you as a borrower that you are paying add-on interest. However, if you are frugal and are trying to get out of debt as well then the simple interest note it the most advantageous for you because no significant savings will be gained by paying the note in full earlier than the maturity date after one-third of the time has lapsed.

Exercise I

Example

An individual borrowed $5,000 for one year at 7% add-on interest but paid the note in full on the date of the fourth monthly payment.
7% add-on is equivalent to 12.68% simple interest.

Rule of 78:

$$\frac{12}{78} + \frac{11}{78} + \frac{10}{78} + \frac{9}{78} = 53.85\%$$ of the total interest due for the year.

$5,000 X .1268 X .5385 = $341.38

Simple Interest:

$$I = P \times R \times T$$

$$= \$5,000 \times 12.68\% \times 4/12 \text{ months}$$

$$= \$5,000 \times .1268 \times .3333$$

$$= \$211.31$$

Savings = $341.38 − $211.31 = $130.07

Using the add-on interest rates shown below and their equivalent simple interest rates, calculate the amount of money the borrower would save by paying the note in 6 months with simple interest rather than add-on interest.

Original Loan	Add-on Rate	Equivalent Simple Rate	Duration of Loan	Interest Saved
$ 500.00	7	12.68	12 mo	
$1,750.00	8	14.45	12 mo	
$3,900.00	9	16.22	12 mo	
$4,100.00	10	17.92	12 mo	
$3,450.00	11	19.57	12 mo	
$7,500.00	12	21.20	12 mo	

Although the examples shown here refer to one individual note, seldom ever would a distributor borrow money to cover a single invoice unless it was an unusually large amount. Even so, many distributors do keep a line of credit at a local lending institution and borrow against that credit when their cash flow is temporarily inadequate to cover their current liabilities. When the accounts receivable come in, they apply these funds to the note in order to stop the interest as soon as possible, as described above.

Chapter 8

Return on Investment

Up to this point we have been discussing the mechanics involved in performing many of the mathematical functions associated with conducting business within the distributorship. At this time let's turn our attention to using all of these things to enhance the profitability of the company. The profitability of the wholesale distributorships is determined by only nine basic things. These include: sales, the cost of goods sold, fixed and variable expenses and personnel. The first four of these are found on the distributor's profit or loss statement. On the balance sheet you find the other four things: inventory, receivables, fixed assets and debt, including both current and long term. Personnel, while very important to profitability will be left for another day.

One of the better methods to use when reviewing the profitability of a distributorship is to input data into the DuPont Return on Investment model, see chart below. When you look at this model which was designed for measuring Return on Investment (ROI) it is apparent that any change, positive or negative, in the values associated with the information in the boxes on the left hand column of the model will affect the ROI.

Therefore, since actions taken by any and all employees in one way or another affect every box in the left hand column, employees need to understand how to impact these things in a positive manner and thus assist in improving the profitability of the company.

Now, let's look more closely at the specific information that needs to be included in the left hand column. The first box to require information is located in the upper left hand corner of the calculator and is marked "sales." In this blank you would record the annual sales figure for the year for which you were calculating the ROI. This figure would be found on the profit or loss statement.

The sales figure is important and most distributors are owned and managed by sales people. They strive for ever and ever higher sales volumes, many time to the demise of their profitability. Should the distributor work to increase sales? Absolutely, if they are profitable sales. If you cannot make money on the sale maybe you should walk away from it. There is always business you cannot afford to take, because it is not profitable. Keep in mind that every action employees take either bring in sales became customers like your service or they drive away sales because of poor service.

The next box on the left hand side of the calculator calls for the cost of goods sold (COGS) to be recorded there. Just as sales affect the ROI so does the cost of goods. If you look at the mathematical formula on the ROI calculator you will notice that when you apply the formula, Sales − COGS, you get the Gross Margin (in dollars). The best profitability goal would be to increase sales while reducing the COGS as a percentage of sales at the same time. If sales were increased say two percent at 25% gross margin, but purchasing could negotiate a volume discount of 2%, then the gross margin would improve from the increased sales and from the reduction in the COGS, both at the same time. This assumes of course that management did not allow sales to pass the lower cost of goods through to the customer in the form of a reduction in the selling price.

The next two boxes on the left hand side of the ROI calculator request information from the profit or loss statement in regard to the fixed and variable expenses. You will note that the formula: gross margin - total expenses, yields the net profit in dollars. Obviously a reduction in either of these categories of expenses, while sales and COGS are constant, would also make a positive impact on the profit of the company. Unfortunately many employees do not understand that if **costs go up** even one dollar then the **profits are reduced** by that same amount. This information should be a significant part of the employee training package.

All of the information discussed above is located on the profit or loss statement and is vitally important to your profitability. The balance sheet is just as important but is all too often overlooked even by some companies who make a good profit. The rule is that you should make as much money from the balance sheet as you do from the P&L. Many managers find this unrealistic. They believe all profits come from sales, and in a sense they do. However, it will become clear how profits can be improved by better management of the balance sheet when we examine the things which make up the Return on Total Assets.

The next box to complete is the one calling for the dollars invested in inventory. (The inventory is know as a current asset because is can be sold and turned into cash in a reasonable period of time.) You should record in the inventory box the average amount of money in dollars invested over the past year in inventory. This is calculated by adding the beginning inventory to the year end inventory and dividing that number by two. The amount of money invested in inventory has a dynamic effect on our profitability. If the inventory is too large it will not turn often enough. This will reduce your profitability. If the inventory is too small, you will not have in stock what the customer wants when it is needed and sales will suffer accordingly. The key is to have a low inventory, of what the customer wants. Therefore, when the inventory is a reasonable size, you have most of the things customers want when they call or come in, yet it is not too large, your profitability will be improved.

The next box to complete is the one for receivables. Record here the average amount of money in dollars your customers owed your company during the year on which the ROI is being calculated. Receivables are also a current asset because they can be collected and turned into cash in a reasonable amount of time, usually 45 to 60 days. The time it takes to turn the receivables into cash is known as "days sales outstanding" or "days receivables." Like the inventory it is important to keep the amount of money invested in receivables low because it affects or profitability by increasing or decreasing the asset turn rate, discussed below.

The next box is the one for cash and other current assets. Record here any money held in checking accounts, savings accounts, certificates of deposit, stocks or bonds or other current assets which are readily convertible to cash. It is important that you have sufficient cash to pay your bills and to grow the business, but excess cash will lower your asset turn rate and will affect your profitability. In any case, very little cash should ever be held in non interest bearing accounts. The rule is "every dollar must be kept working every hour of ever day" (and night for that matter). So if the money is not working in the business then it should at least be drawing interest.

The next box that you need to complete is the one for fixed assets. They are also found on the balance sheet. Find the number and record it in the proper space. The general rule is that distributors should not own property. They should lease it. This principle leads many owners of distributorships, who do want to own property, to buy land and buildings and lease them back to the distributorship at fair market value. This method allows the owner to fairly evaluate the return being made on the money invested strictly in the distribution portion of the business without distorting the number by the value of land and buildings; which would also be included if owned by the company.

Recorded at strategic locations on the ROI calculator you will find the necessary formulas which tell you how to calculate the numbers which belong in the other boxes. Using the data from the P&L and the balance sheet fill in the proper boxes. For all others, use the formulas, calculate the information and record it in the remaining boxes.

The management of sales as well as the money invested in the company, including all of the things discussed above, is customarily the responsibility of the company's branch managers. This person would be held accountable for the sales, COGS, expenses, inventory and receivables. (Most branch managers are not responsible for cash, except petty cash, because the customers pay their invoices directly to the corporate office.) Let's look then at how the effectiveness of the branch manager should be measured and upon what measures his/her performance should be rewarded.

When you follow the numbers you have recorded across the calculator from left to right you will find that the items from the P&L culminate in the box "Net Profit on Sales." The numbers from the balance sheet would include: inventory, receivables, petty cash and fixed assets and culminate in the box entitled "Asset Turnover."

You will recall that you can make money from both the P&L and the balance sheet. This is true because the asset turnover from the balance sheet is a multiplier against the net profit on sales which together determine how much money the branch manager made with the assets entrusted to his or her care, the total assets. It should be clear then that the "Return on Total Assets" is the number for which the branch managers should be held responsible and on which they should be rewarded, good or bad.

The last two boxes, on the left hand side near the bottom of the ROI calculator, that need to be completed are titled Current Liabilities (money you owe your suppliers and lenders for short term notes) and long term debt. These are both controlled by the owner or corporate manager and are not the responsibility of the branch manager. The branch manager cannot tell corporate management when to pay the company's bills (payables) nor can he/she tell them how much money to borrow.

These two items, current liabilities and long term debt, are factors which determine the financial leverage of the company. The more highly leveraged the company is the higher will be the ROI. It sounds reasonable then that companies should owe a great deal of money; be highly leveraged. This in not a sound philosophy in the distribution business because the owners are also vulnerable to the next economic down turn. When the economy turns down, which it does on a regular basis, the distributor which is highly leveraged may not have enough cash to pay employees, current bills and pay the interest and principle due on a large bank note. When this happens the company goes broke quickly. Leverage factors in the range of 1.5 to 2.5 are generally acceptable for profitable distributorships.

Now, let's discuss the other factor important to all distributor owners. Most owners want to know how much money they made with the capital they had invested in the company, know as the owner's net worth. The net worth is calculated by subtracting the total debt from the total assets of the company. The total assets reveal to you the total worth of the company. When you subtract the amount owed to others, payables and long term debt, you find the amount of the company which belongs to the owners, called net worth.

The net worth when divided into the total assets determines the financial leverage of the company, as previously discussed. The only good leverage to have is located in "trade payables" (the amount of money owed to your suppliers). Why? Because this is the only interest free debt you have. When this type debt is high you are leveraging your company with an interest free loan from the manufacturers you represent. The leverage tells corporation managers how well they are using borrowed monies to enhance the ROI.

In summary, branch managers should be rewarded for how well they performed with the assets entrusted to their care which is depicted in the return on total assets. Corporate managers should be rewarded on how well they supported the branch managers in addition to how much money they made with the leverage factor. The return on total assets multiplied times the leverage factor yields the ROI, the number upon which the professional corporate manager should be rewarded.

ROI CALCULATOR

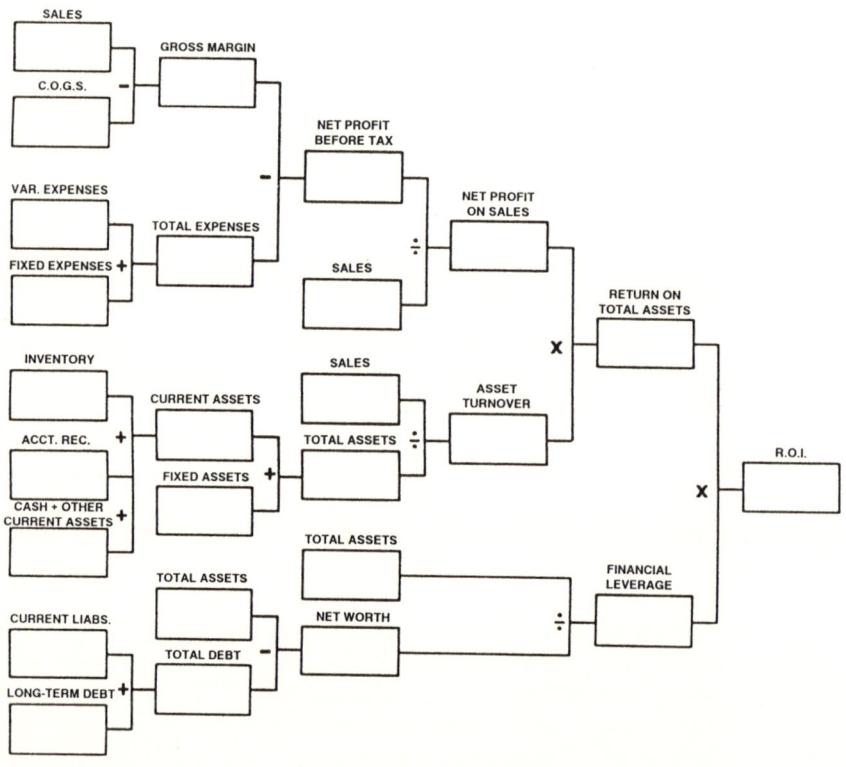

Answer Key

The problems in the exercises of this book are worked out for you in this section. Where exercises are in Table form, one or more examples are worked and the answer provided for the remainder of the problems.

All word (statement) problems are worked out in detail.

CHAPTER THREE: PERCENTAGES IN WHOLESALING

3.1 CALCULATING THE PERCENT

1) 1/5 = 0.2 × 100 = 20%
2) 1/4 = 0.25 × 100 = 25%
3) 33%
4) 43%
5) 80%
6) 44%
7) 62%
8) 75%
9) 14%
10) 8%
11) 81%
12) 63%
13) 30%
14) 24%
15) 90%

3.2 CALCULATING THE PERCENTAGE

PERCENTAGE = RATE × BASE

EXERCISE I

1) 25% of $1,500 = 0.25 × 1,500 = $375.00
2) 18% of $1,278 = 0.18 × 1,278 = $230.04
3) $ 86.25
4) $ 377.57
5) $ 1,392.00
6) $ 7,875.00
7) $18,342.00
8) $ 546.36
9) $ 5,840.00
10) $ 101.07
11) $ 2.50
12) $ 0.15
13) $ 4.63
14) $ 0.14

EXERCISE II

Calculate the percentage in the following simple statement problems.

1) 35% of 123 = 0.35 × 123 = 43.05
2) 300% of 444 = 3.00 × 444 = 1,332.00
3) 3/10% of 115 = 0.003 × 115 = 0.345

4) 18% of 40 = 0.18 × 40 = 7.20
5) 7% of 49 = 0.07 × 49 = 3.43

EXERCISE III

Calculate the percentage in the following complex statement problems.

1) 0.05 × $1,250,000 = $62,500
2) 0.05 × ($650,000 − $500,000) = $7,500
3) machinery = 0.60 × $520,000 = $312,000
   fixtures = (100% − 60%) × $520,000 = $208,000
4) "A" = [100% − (23% + 32%)] × $53,000 = $23,850
   "B" = 0.32 × $53,000 = $16,960
   "C" = 0.23 × $53,000 = $12,190
5) A) 0.18 × $580,000 = $104,400
   B) 0.18 × $730,000 = $131,400
6) 0.08 × $18,000 = $1,440
7) 0.21 × $780,000 = $163,800
8) 0.08 × $86,000 = $6,880
9) (0.27 × $29,000) × (100% − 78%) = $1,722.60

3.3 CALCULATING THE RATE

R = P ÷ B

EXERCISE I

Calculate the rate when the percentage and base are known.

1) 0.79 ÷ $8 = 9.88%
2) 0.75 ÷ 0.85 = 88.24%
3) 18 ÷ 28 = 64.29%
4) 35 ÷ 53 = 66.04%
5) 12. ÷ 1/4 = 5,000.00%
6) 0.60 ÷ 1/2 = 120.00%
7) 0.52 ÷ 9/16 = 92.44%
8) $25 ÷ $75 = 33.33%
9) $85 ÷ $190 = 44.14%
10) $80 ÷ $104 = 76.92%
11) $68 ÷ $223 = 30.49%
12) $30 ÷ $241 = 12.45%
13) $70 ÷ $75 = 93.33%
14) $11 ÷ $150 = 7.33%
15) $46 ÷ $57 = 80.70%

EXERCISE II

Calculate the rate of these simple statement problems.

1) 51 ÷ 85 = 60.00%
2) 23 ÷ 68 = 33.82%
3) 62 ÷ 52 = 119.23%
4) 270 ÷ 156 = 173.08%
5) 4,863 ÷ 10,816 = 44.96%

EXERCISE III

Calculate the rate of these complex statement problems.

1. A) [($12,500 − $10,000) ÷ $12,500] × 100 = 20%
   B) $10,000 ÷ $12,500 = 80% or 100% − 20% = 80%

2. A) 120 ÷ (120 + 67) = 64.17%
   B) 67 ÷ 187 = 35.83%

3) A) "A" = $1,579,200 ÷ $6,580,000 = 24%
   B) "B" = $1,217,300 ÷ $6,580,000 = 18.50%

4 A) ($2,250 − $1,500) ÷ $2,250 = 33.33%
   B) ($750 − $250) ÷ $2,250 = 22.22%

5) Yes
   $8,400 − [($8,400 × 0.20) × 2] = $5,040 Book Value
   $5,040 − $3,640 = $1,400 loss on sale

3.4 CALCULATING THE BASE

B = P ÷ R

EXERCISE I

Calculate the base when the percentage and rate are given.

1) 64 ÷ 0.16 = 400.00
2) 39 ÷ 0.32 = 121.88
3) 334 ÷ 0.2 = 1,151.72
4) 8 ÷ 0.02 = 400.00
5) 11 ÷ 0.04 = 275.00
6) 573 ÷ 0.09 = 6,366.67
7) 60 ÷ 0.075 = 800.00
8) 27 ÷ 0.0925 = 291.89
9) 75 ÷ 0.0667 = 1,124.44
10) 97 ÷ 1.19 = 81.51
11) 72 ÷ 1.80 = 40.00
12) 43 ÷ 2.19 = 19.63
13) 19.5 ÷ 1.17 = 16.67
14) 1.5 ÷ 0.085 = 17.65
15) 3.05 ÷ 1.18 = 2.58

EXERCISE II

Calculate the base in these simple statement problems.

1) 800 ÷ 0.40 = 2,000
2) 10 ÷ 0.025 = 400
3) 15 ÷ 0.30 = 50
4) 45 ÷ 0.08 = 562.5
5) 75 ÷ 1.50 = 50

EXERCISE III

Calculate the base when the percentage and rate are given.

1) $4,991 \div 0.23 = \$21,700$

2) $7,012.50 \div 0.1375 = \$51,000$

3) A) $8,800 \div 0.16 = \$55,000$
   B) $8,800 \times 6 = \$52,800$

4) $165 \div (100\% - 40\%) = \$275$

5 A) $19,895 \div 0.23 = \$86,500$
   B) $86,500 \times 0.06 = \$5,190$

6) $19,177 \div 0.25 = \$76,708$

7) $4,000 \div 0.165 = \$24,242.42$

8) $14,342 \div 0.60 = \$23,903.33$

9) $16,500 \div (100\% - 12.50\%) = \$18,857.14$

3.5 PERCENT OF CHANGE BETWEEN NUMBERS

EXERCISE I

Calculate the percent change in these simple statement problems.

1) $(1,400 - 1,200 \div 1,200) \times 100 = 16.67\%$
2) $(\$81,000 - \$70,000 \div \$81,000) \times 100 = 13.58\%$
3) $(180 - 120 \div 120) \times 100 = 50\%$
4) $(\$695 - \$400 \div \$695) \times 100 = 42.45\%$

EXERCISE II

1) $28,965 × 1.15 × 1.15 × 1.15 × 1.15 = $50,659.97
2) $23,685 × 1.08 × 1.08 × 1.08 = $29,836.28
3) $40,000 × 1.02 × 1.08 × 1.12 = $49,351.68
4) $9,500 × 0.50 × 0.75 × 0.92 × 0.92 = $3,015.30
5) $69,578 × 1.08 × 1.08 × 1.08 × 0.88 × 1.04 × 1.04 × 1.04 = $86,761.27

EXERCISE III

1) Total = 540 tons = 100%
   25 × $2,450 = $61,250
   [(540 − 25) × 0.50] × $1,800 = $463,500
   [257.5 × (100% − 75%)] × $1,150 = $74,031.25
   Total Received = $598,781.25
   Unsold (257.5 × .75) / 540 = 35.76%

2) "A" = $51,000 × 0.015 = $765
   "B" = $17,500 × 0.02 = $350
   "C" = $5,000 × 0.03 = $150
   Total Commission = $1,265

3) "A" = $47,500 × 0.015 = $712.50
   "B" = $15,000 × 0.02 = $300.00
   "C" = $3,500 × 0.03 = $105.00
   Total Commission = $1,117.50

4) Total = 84 tons = 100%
   (84 × 0.60) × $1,750 = $88,200
   [84 × (100% − 60%)] × 0.75 × $1,400 = $35,280

[33.6 × (100% − 75%)] × $900 = $7,560
Total Money = $131,040

5) $75,000 − $60,250 = $14,750 Difference
$14,750 × 0.02 = $295.00 Short this month

6) Total Sales = $300,000 = 100%
Abrasives = $300,000 × 0.35 = $105,000
Hand Tools = $300,000 × 0.10 = $30,000
Electrical Goods = [$300,000 × (100% − 35% − 10%)] × 0.75 = $123,750
General Maintenance = $300,000 × 0.55 × (100% − 75%) = $41,250

7) Total = 240 = 100%
240 × 0.479 × $95 = $10,921.20
[240 × (100% − 47.9%)] × 0.64 × $83.50 = $6,682.14
[240 × 0.521 × (100% − 64%)] × $67.50 = $3,038.47
Total Received = $20,641.81

8) Total = 27,000 = 100%
27,000 × 0.42 × $12 = $136,080
27,000 × 0.10 × $9.95 = $26,865
27,000 × (100% − 52%) × 0.60 × $8.95 = $69,595.20
Total Received = $232,540.20
27,000 × 0.48 × (100% − 60%) = 5184 unsold
5,184 ÷ 27,000 = 19.2% unsold

9) Total = $105,000 = 100%
$105,000 × (100% − 27% − 60%) = $13,650 left

10) Total = 17,000 = 100%
17,000 × 0.65 × $2.95 = $32,597.50
17,000 × 0.10 × $2.15 = $3,655.00
17,000 × (100% − 65% − 10%) × $1.44 = $6,120.00 loss
Total Received = $32,597.50 + $3,655.00 = $36,252.50

Loss = $6,120.00
Lost Income = $6,120.00 ÷ $36,252.50 X 100 = 16.88%

11) [($250,000 − $180,000) X 0.03] + $18,000 + $600 = $20,700

12) $380 X (100% − 22%) = $296.40

13) [($364,000 X 0.75) ÷ 100] X $0.80 = $2,184

14) Cost = 50% of the Loss
Cost = 50% of the Selling Price
Loss is 100% of the Selling Price.

CHAPTER FOUR: DISCOUNTS

4.2 SIMPLIFIED METHOD

EXERCISE I

Find the invoice price of the following items and the dollar amount of the discount:

Item	List Price	Lead Disc. %	Second Disc. %	Invoice Amount	Discount Allowed (In $)
1.	$ 20	10	0	$ 18.00	$ 2.00
2.	$ 40	9	0	$ 36.40	$ 3.60
3.	$ 93	15	0	$ 79.05	$ 13.95
4.	$ 61	29	0	$ 43.31	$ 17.69
5.	$973	16.5	0	$812.46	$160.54
6.	$127	8.25	0	$116.52	$ 10.48
7.	$213	28.75	0	$151.76	$ 61.24
8.	$ 55	10	10	$ 44.55	$ 10.45
9.	$584	12	8	$472.81	$111.19
10.	$323	33	6	$203.43	$119.57
11.	$270	14	1	$229.89	$ 40.12
12.	$330	5	.5	$311.93	$ 18.07
13.	$818	50	5	$388.55	$429.45
14.	$439	2.5	2.25	$418.39	$ 20.61
15.	$ 91	3.5	.5	$ 87.38	$ 3.62

4.3 ALTERNATE METHOD

EXERCISE I

Calculate and record single unit multipliers, invoice amounts and trade discounts received in the problems given below.

Item	List Price	Trade Disc. %	Multi-plying Factor	Inv. Amt.	Disc. Rec'd.
1.			.7220	$ 36.10	13.90
2.			.8123	$ 60.92	14.08
3.			.8024	$ 80.24	19.76
4.			.8678	$1,333.00	203.00
5.			.9154	$2,342.40	216.60
6.			.7016	$4,380.04	1,862.96
7.			.5544	$2,116.70	1,701.30
8.			.9411	$ 112.93	7.07
9.			.5530	$ 311.87	252.13
10.			.4631	$3,692.03	4,279.97

4.4 MULTIPLIER FACTORS

EXERCISE I

Calculate for each of the following problems: 1) The amount of the invoice 2) The amount of the discount. 3) The multiplying factor.

1) $4.00 X 0.845 X 0.90 = $3.04
    1) $3.04
    2) $0.96
    3) .7605

2) $460 X 0.84 X 0.86 = $332.30
    1) $332.30

2) $127.70
3) .7224

3) $3400 × (10,000 ÷ 100) × 0.78 × 0.83 × 0.975 × 0.975 = $209,236
   1) $209,247.77
   2) $130,752.23
   3) .6154

4) $86,500 × 0.75 × 0.95 × 0.99 × 0.995 = $60,709.86
   1) $60,709.86
   2) $25,790.14
   3) .7018

5) $1,500 × 0.70 × 0.92 × 0.9688 = $935.86
   Disc. = $564.14
   $180 × 0.75 × 0.9575 × 0.9825 = $127.00
   Disc. = $53.00

EXERCISE II

1) Purchase Price =
   $460 × 0.74 × 0.8575 = $291.89
   Selling Price = $460 × 0.82 × 0.93 = $350.80
   Gross Margin = $350.80 − $291.89 = $58.91

2) $18.50 × 0.79 × 0.89 = $13.01/case
   $22.50/12 = $1.88 freight/case
   Total Cost = $13.01 + $1.88 = $14.89/case

3) A discount of 40% and 10%
   25%, 20%, 5%   0.75 × 0.80 × 0.95 = 0.57
   $360 × 0.57 = $205.20
   40%, 10%   0.60 × 0.90 = 0.54
   $360 × 0.54 = $194.40
   Savings = $10.80

4) $96 ÷ $128 = 75%   100% − 75% = 25%
   Trade Discount = 25%

5) $179 X 0.75 X Additional Discount = $120
   Additional Discount = 0.8939
   100% − 89.39% = 10.61% Trade Discount

6) ($245.00 X 0.75 X 0.8) − Additional Discount = $122.50
   Change = $147 − $122.50 = $24.50
   $24.50 ÷ $147 X 100% = 16.67%

7) 0.80 X 0.85 X 0.95 = 0.85 X 0.95 X 0.80   0.646 = 0.646
   Commutative Law

8) $24.95/case X 0.82 X 0.91 X 0.965 = $17.97/case
   ($24.95 ÷ 24)/tube X 0.82 X 0.91 X 0.965 = $0.75/tube
   $24.95 case ÷ $1.04 tube is approximately equal to $17.97 case ÷ $0.75 tube

9) Purchase 10
   1 - 9 units $218 X 0.70 = $152.60 each
   10 - 15 units $218 X 0.70 X 0.90 = $137.34 each
   $152.60 X 9 = $1,373.40 total cost
   $137.34 X 10 = $1,373.40 total cost
   Buy 10 – get one free with the bigger discount.

10) 1) $56 X 0.75 X 0.90 X 0.95 X 0.95 = $34.11/foot
    2) $56 X 8900   = $498,400 without discount
       $56 X 0.6092   = $34.11/foot X 8,900 feet = $303,619.05
       Total Discount = $498,400 − $303,619.05 = $194,780.95
    3) $195,780.95 ÷ $498,400 = 39.08%

5.4 CASH DISCOUNTS

EXERCISE I

Calculate the cash discount offered and taken as stated in the next problems.

Item	Invoice Amount	Disc. Terms	Inv. Date	Date Paid	Discount Offered
1.	$1,790				$1,772.10
2.	$7,194				$7,050.12
3.	$5,468				$5,358.64
4.	$2,594				$2,594.00
5.	$ 135				$ 134.33

EXERCISE II

1) July has 31 days so 31 − 28 = 3
   3 + 8 = 11 days
   11 > 10 so bill must be paid in full.

2) 31 − 22 = 9   9 + 2 = 11
   $2,303.28 X 0.985 = $2,268.73 Net Payment

3) 31 − 28 = 3   3 + 7 = 10
   $34,500 X 0.03 = $1,035 Discount Offered

4) 28 − 20 = 8   8 + 1 = 9
   $1,195 X 0.025 = $29.88 Discount Offered
   $1,195 X 0.975 = $1,165.12 Net Payment

5) 15 − 1 = 14 $1,220 X 0.99 = $1,207.80

6) 31 − 27 = 4   4 + 7 = 11   No Disc.
   Payment = $7,850.75

7) 31 − 26 = 5   5 + 6 = 11
   $1,083.75 X 0.99 = $1,072.91

8) 31 − 21 = 10   10 + 1 = 11
$7,800 × 0.02 = $156 Discount
$7,800 × 0.98 = $7,644 Amount Paid
If payment Oct. 31: Discount 3%

5.8 COMBINATION PROBLEMS

EXERCISE I

1) $2,300 × 0.98 = $2,254
$2,254 ÷ 100 = $22.54/wheel

2) $150 × 10 = $1,500 list
$1,500 × 0.82 × 0.78 × 0.97 = $930.62 paid on May 14
Multiplier = .6396
$930.62 × (0.11 × 45) ÷ 365 = $12.62 interest
$1,500 × 0.82 × 0.78 = $959.40
$959.40 − ($930.62 + $12.62) = $16.16 savings

3) $95,785 × 0.85 × 0.9 × 0.95 × 0.975 × 0.98 = $66,514.03

4) $52,021 × 0.89 × 0.93 × 0.99 = $42,627.20 invoice
$42,627.20 in full
$42,627.20 × 0.975 = $41,561.52
($41,561.52 × 0.015 × 12 × 75) ÷ 365 = $1,537.21 Interest
$41,561.52 + $1,537.21 = $43,098.73 Loan
$42,627.20 × 0.025 = $1,065.68 Disc.   Loan > Invoice
Interest > Discount   No, do not borrow

5) 5 packages × 4 units × $118.50/unit
× 0.95 × 0.975 × 0.975 = $2,140.33 Invoice
Multiplier = .9031
$2,370 List - $2,140.33 Invoice =
$229.67 Trade Discount
$229.67 ÷ $2,370 = 9.69% Trade Disc.
$2,140.33 × 0.02 = $42.81 Cash Disc.
Interest > Discount
Contractor would not save money

CHAPTER SIX: MARKUPS

6.1 FINDING THE PERCENT GROSS MARGIN WHEN THE PERCENT MARKUP IS KNOWN

$$PGM = \frac{\text{Percent Markup}}{100\% + \text{Percent Markup}} \times 100$$

EXERCISE I

Using the formula for calculating the percent gross margin when the percent markup is known, calculate the percent gross margin on the following:

Percent Markup	Percent Gross Margin
11.11	10
17.65	15
25.00	20
33.33	25
42.86	30
53.86	35
66.67	40
80.00	45
100.00	50

6.2 FINDING PERCENT MARKUP WHEN THE PERCENT GROSS MARGIN IS KNOWN

$$\text{Percent Markup} = \frac{PGM}{100 - PGM} \times 100$$

EXERCISE I

Using the formula for finding the percent markup when the desired percent gross margin is known, calculate the percent markups in the following problems.

Desired Percent Gross Margin	Percent Markup
9	10.00
11	12.36
12	13.64
16	19.05
18	21.95
26	35.14
32	47.06
46	85.19

EXERCISE II

Using the formulas for percent markup, calculate the percent markup, the markup in dollars and the selling price of the following items.

COGS	Percent Gross Margin	Percent Markup	Markup in Dollars	Selling Price
$ 100	20	25.00	$ 25.00	$ 125.00
$ 119	18	21.95	$ 26.12	$ 145.12
$ 644	9	9.89	$ 63.69	$ 707.69
$5,282	13.5	15.61	$ 824.52	$ 6,106.52
$ 755	27	36.99	$ 279.27	$ 1,034.27
$9,576	31	44.93	$4,302.50	$13,878.50
$ 813	38	61.29	$ 498.29	$ 1,311.29
$ 227	5.25	5.54	$ 12.58	$ 239.58
$3,691	49	96.08	$3,546.31	$ 7,237.31

EXERCISE III

1) Percent Markup = (0.05 ÷ 0.95)(100) = 5.26%
   Selling Price = (0.0526 × $118,000)
   + $118,000 = $124,206.80

2) Percent Markup = (0.09 ÷ 0.91)(100) = 9.89%
   Markup = $142.00 (0.0989) = $14.04

3) Percent Markup = (0.28 ÷ 0.72)(100) = 38.89%
   Markup = $701.00 (0.3889) = $272.62
   Selling Price = $701.00 + $272.62 = $973.62

4) Percent Markup = (0.21 ÷ 0.79)(100) = 26.58%
   Selling Price = $57.00 (0.2658) + 57.00 = $72.15/case
   $72.15 × 30 = $2,164.50 for 30 cases

5) Motor Percent Markup = (0.25 ÷ 0.75)(100) = 33.33%
   Selling Price = ($81.00 × 0.3333) + $81.00 = $108.00
   Compressor Percent Markup = (0.18 ÷ 0.82) × 100 = 21.95%
   Selling Price = (730.00 × 0.2195) + $730 = $890.24
   Tank Percent Markup = (0.20 ÷ 0.80)(100) = 25%
   Selling Price = ($316.00 × 0.25) + $316.00 = $395.00
   Combined Selling Price = $1,393.24

6.3 CALCULATING THE PERCENT MARKUP WHEN THE COGS AND SELLING PRICE ARE KNOWN

$$\text{Percent Markup} = \frac{\text{Selling Price} - \text{COGS}}{\text{COGS}} \times 100$$

EXERCISE I

Using the formula for calculating the percent markup when the COGS and selling price are known, calculate the percent markup in each of the following.

Selling Price	COGS	Percent Markup
$ 150.00	$100.00	50.00%
$ 10.00	$8.10	23.46%
$1,140.25	$1,000.00	14.03%
$ 980.17	$615.90	59.14%
$ 712.00	$436.49	63.12%
$3,960.69	$2,999.99	32.02%
$ 4.25	$2.10	111.44%
$ 11.79	$3.50	236.86%
$2,466.38	$2,155.25	14.44%
$ 800.00	$715.00	11.89%

6.4 CALCULATING THE SELLING PRICE FROM THE COST OF GOODS USING THE DIVISOR PRINCIPLE

$$\text{Selling Price} = \frac{\text{COGS}}{100\% - \text{Percent Gross Margin}}$$

EXERCISE I

Calculate and insert below the proper "divisors" required to ascertain the selling price when the COGS and the desired percent gross margin are known.

Desired Percent Gross Margin	Divisor	COGS	Selling Price
5.00%	.95	$ 149	$ 156.84
7.50%	.925	$ 388	$ 419.46
11.00%	.89	$ 955	$1,073.03
14.00%	.86	$ 251	$ 291.86
20.00%	.80	$7,591	$9,488.75
31.33%	.6867	$4,472	$6,512.31
37.00%	.63	$1,873	$2,973.02
40.00%	.60	$ 776	$1,293.33
41.375%	.5863	$ 339	$ 578.20
25.00%	.75	$ 314	$ 418.67

EXERCISE II

Make a chart and insert the divisors which an employee could use to find the selling price of any item with gross margins between 18 and 25 percent. Use only whole percentage points.

Gross Margin	Divisor
18	.82
19	.81
20	.80
21	.79
22	.78
23	.77
24	.76
25	.75

6.6 CALCULATING MULTIPLE MARKUPS FROM COST

EXERCISE I

1) Selling Price = $25 ÷ 0.82 = $30.49

2) Selling Price = $83 ÷ 0.60 = $138.33

3) Selling Price = $175 ÷ 0.685 = 255.47

4) Selling Price = $170 ÷ 0.7375 = $230.51

5) Selling Price = $75,750 ÷ 0.77 = $98,376.62
   Gross Margin = 98,376.62 − $75,750 = $22,626.62

6) Selling Price = $856.50 ÷ 0.8267 = $1,036.05
   Gross Margin = $1,036.05 − $856.50 = $179.55

7) Selling Price = $17,693 ÷ 0.9333 = $18,957.46
   Gross Margin = $18,957.46 − $17,693 = $1,264.46

8) List Price = $87,500 ÷ 0.625 = $140,000
   Discount = $140,000 − $87,500 = $52,500

9) List Price = $1,623 ÷ 0.18 = $9,016.67
   = $9,016.67 ÷ 0.80 = $11,270.83
   Selling Price = $9,016.67

10) (3 X $24,000) ÷ (0.85 X 0.95)
    = $72,000 ÷ 0.8075
    = $89,164.09 List Price
    $89,164.09 X 0.85 = $75,789.48
    $75,789.48 X 0.05 = $3,789.47 Savings

11) $78.50 ÷ (0.80 X 0.95) = $103.29 each
    $75.00 ÷ (0.80 X 0.95 X 0.955)
    = $103.33 each
    $103.31 X 0.85 = $87.81 customer costs on both units
    $78.50 − $75.00 = $3.50 difference on each sale

12) Net Price = $9,572 ÷ 0.83 = $11,532.53
    List Price = $11,532.53 ÷ (0.85 X 0.95 X 0.98) = $14,572.31
    Discounts = $14,572.31 − $11,532.53 = $3,039.78

CHAPTER SEVEN: INTEREST ON BORROWED MONEY

7.1 SIMPLE INTEREST FORMULA

$I = P \times R \times T$

EXERCISE I

Find the amount of interest a distributor must pay on each of the following loans and calculate the total amount owed on the date of payment.

Amount	%	# Days	Interest	Amount Due
$ 750	5	365	$ 37.50	$ 787.50
$ 900	6	90	$ 13.32	$ 913.32
$ 1,215	7.50	45	$ 11.23	$ 1,226.23
$18,518	10.25	180	$963.14	$19,454.14
$ 6,637	8.375	210	$319.80	$ 6,956.80
$ 5,000	14	480	$920.54	$ 5,920.54
$ 6,000	6	60	$ 59.18	$ 6,059.18
$ 381	18	30	$ 5.64	$ 386.64
$ 8,163	12.125	310	$840.62	$ 9,003.62
$ 900	16.50	115	$ 46.79	$ 946.79

7.2 SINGLE PAYMENT NOTES

EXERCISE I

Calculate the total interest paid on the following notes:

Original Loan	Annual Rate %	First Payment Amount Paid	First Payment Days Held	2nd Payment Amt. Paid	2nd Payment Days Held	Total Interest
$ 5,000	10	$ 2,000	15	$ 3,000	60	$ 69.87
$ 819	9	$ 819	75			$ 15.15
$ 1,274	12	$ 637	180	$ 6,373	60	$ 150.79
$28,010	9.5	$ 8,010	60	$20,000	90	$ 905.91
$ 7,500	11.125	$ 2,500	36	$ 5,000	58	$ 170.68
$89,890	8.75	$46,000	40	$43,890	80	$1,703.69
$ 3,115	14	$1,000	10	$ 2,115	180	$ 157.97
$ 1,790	13.33	$ 1,790	90			$ 58.85
$14,212	18	$10,000	27	$ 4,212	42	$ 276.41
$ 3,600	8.25	$ 600	15	$ 3,000	45	$ 42.72

7.3 ADD-ON INTEREST

EXERCISE I

Original Loan	Add-on Rate	Equivalent Simple Rate	Duration of Loan	Interest Saved
$ 500	7	12.68	12 mths.	$ 14.63
$1,750	8	14.45	"	$ 58.34
$3,900	9	16.22	"	$145.94
$4,100	10	17.92	"	$169.50
$3,450	11	19.57	"	$155.76
$7,500	12	21.20	"	$366.81

The Author

Dr. Rice has the honor of receiving a "Distinguished Teaching Award" from the Texas A&M Association of Former Students as he is an internationally known professor of continuing education, a noted author, lecturer, and consultant in the field of distribution management.

Dr. Rice was formerly the Director of the Thomas A. Read Center for Distribution Research and Education at Texas A&M University and was Coordinator of the Industrial Distribution for 25 years.

He is the author of nine books, including such topics as the total quality process, financial transactions of the wholesale distributor, planning and managing the distributorship for greater profit, the wholesale distributor purpose and functions, challenges facing distributors and finances in the Christian home. In addition to his books he has authored more than 60+ trade journal articles, some of which have been incorporated into a book of readings.

Dr. Rice served two terms on the Governor's Council for Quality Texas where he and his colleagues were responsible for developing the Quality Process Awareness curriculum for businesses in Texas with less than 500 employees.

The Council of Fleet Specialties named their most prestigious "quality award" to honor Dr. Rice, in 1997.

In 1990 he was listed first among the top 20 most influential people in the electrical industry by *Electrical Wholesaling* magazine.

He had the honor of holding the J. R. Thompson Endowed Professorship in Distribution Management, named for Dick Thompson, his close friend and mentor for many years.

NOTES

NOTES

NOTES

NOTES

NOTES